"Bringing best practices of leac
Leadership Roundtable since it.
to support those men nearing o
vital way in parish life."

    —Rev. Renato J. Bautista, Director of Formation
    Immaculate Conception Seminary School of Theology
    West Orange, New Jersey

"This book is a timely and valuable resource for seminary rectors and formators
to prepare and implement the changes to pastoral formation required by the
new *Program of Priestly Formation*, and to equip newly ordained priests to
assume future responsibilities as pastors."

    —Rev. Andrew Turner, Rector of Saint Mary Seminary
    Cleveland, Ohio

"There is a direct link to parish vitality and those in leadership. At times, priests
stumble in the basics of leadership, and this book offers a broad spectrum
of sound advice and wisdom to strengthen and augment their skills as they
transition from being seminarians to the gift and challenge of priestly ministry.
The whole people of God can benefit from our priests being well-informed
leaders who are open to ongoing formation from the authors of this book who
are experts in their fields."

    —Bishop David L. Toups
    Diocese of Beaumont, Texas

"The revised *Program of Priestly Formation* identifies four stages of
propaedeutic, discipleship, configuration, and vocational synthesis. Leadership
Roundtable has responded to this with a text targeted for seminarians as they
prepare to transition from seminary to parish and priestly service. I commend
them for their vision and support of the church."

    —Cardinal Joseph Tobin
    Archdiocese of Newark, New Jersey

A Seminarian's Toolbox

Preparing for Parish Leadership

Edited by Patrick Stokely

LITURGICAL PRESS
Collegeville, Minnesota

litpress.org

© 2024 by Leadership Roundtable
Published by Liturgical Press, Collegeville, Minnesota. All rights reserved. No part of this book may be used or reproduced in any manner whatsoever, except brief quotations in reviews, without written permission of Liturgical Press, Saint John's Abbey, PO Box 7500, Collegeville, MN 56321-7500. Printed in the United States of America.

1	2	3	4	5	6	7	8	9

Library of Congress Cataloging-in-Publication Control Number: 2023043434

ISBN 978-0-8146-6775-0
ISBN 978-0-8146-6776-7 (e-book)

Contents

Foreword

Kevin C. Kennedy

Happy are those who find wisdom,
*   and those who get understanding,*
for her income is better than silver,
*   and her revenue better than gold.*
She is more precious than jewels,
*   and nothing you desire can compare with her.*
Long life is in her right hand;
*   in her left hand are riches and honor.*
Her ways are ways of pleasantness,
*   and all her paths are peace.*
She is a tree of life to those who lay hold of her;
*   those who hold her fast are called happy.*

Proverbs 3:13-18

Pursuing wisdom is the lifelong endeavor you began through years of study, prayer, and pastoral experience in seminary. Applying what you learned in the initial years after ordination is critical to crystallizing your priesthood. The many themes in this book, combined with the guidance of mentors, will assist you in discerning and preparing to become a pastor. As you know, despite your years in the seminary, there is still much to learn. But don't let that frustrate you. See it as a lifelong adventure to understand yourself, build your capacity to serve others, and deepen your relationship with God. Embracing an open attitude to continuous learning will give you the confidence to lead and live well.

You may have heard some of these before: "I am a lawyer, but not yet a partner; a police officer, but just a rookie; a doctor, but still a resident; a priest, though just an associate." The "already-but-not-yet" paradigm is common to most careers and vocations. There are many paths a recently ordained priest might travel, with decisions and formative moments along the way. Mentor priests and parishioners offer direction for ministry in administration, education, chaplaincy, and pastoring a parish. Many priests become pastors faster than lawyers make partner, medical residents become certified specialists, or rookies become veteran cops. Thus, the skills and insights you obtain in your initial assignment are critical for your proficiency.

Mentors understand their role in helping translate book knowledge into practical wisdom for a recently ordained priest. Good mentors, co-workers in ministry, and the parish community will offer you guidance and sufficient latitude to grow into the pastor role. People are rooting for your success. This book is an excellent complement to those other sources of support, especially in developing your leadership and management capacity. Refer to this book often in your initial years of priesthood and discuss the concepts with your mentors. Use it as a "toolbox" from which you can choose and apply the appropriate tool to your situation. The self-discovery of your aptitude for leadership and administration can be exciting as you reflect upon the kind of leader you are becoming. This toolbox will help you explore questions such as: "How might my strengths be nurtured, my areas of weakness be addressed, and my idiosyncrasies be moderated as I collaborate with others?" The content of this book and the experience you gather from pastoral ministry will augment the years of formation you received through your seminary experience. While you are not yet a pastor, you have so much to give and so much to gain. God bless you in this endeavor.

Introduction

Patrick Markey

"The whole journey of life is a journey of preparation" (Pope Francis).

These words from the Holy Father set up beautifully the purpose of this work titled *A Seminarian's Toolbox: Preparing for Parish Leadership*.

If you are reading this book, you are most likely preparing to enter a new, exciting, and important phase in your life as a Catholic priest. The call to the ministerial priesthood is as deeply personal as it is communal. Personally you are studying, deepening your relationship with Jesus who has called you, and reflecting on what it means to live a life of service. You are also preparing to work with and within a community of believers, the church in which you will most likely immerse yourself through a parish.

While your time in the seminary is preparing you for much of this, built into your preparation for ministry is a good deal of learning on the job after the seminary. In years past, a newly ordained priest had time and opportunities to learn the rhythm of parish life and the roles and responsibilities that come with being a pastor—a job most of you one day will be called to do. Most often the rookie priest was placed in a parish with a seasoned priest who as pastor would mentor his younger colleague and teach him the ropes. It was normal, in those times, for a priest to be an associate pastor as long as ten years before being given charge of a parish.

Well, those days are gone. Unfortunately, in the current reality of the church in many parts of the world there is not the time or personnel for that important mentorship. More and more, newly ordained priests are finding themselves as leaders of important ministries, most often in parishes, without the benefit of on-the-ground training. How can we avoid or at least minimize the potential mishaps that could happen (and are happening!) during this on-the-job training period? This is one of the areas where Leadership Roundtable can be of immeasurable assistance.

As you have been prayerfully discerning the call to priesthood, this book is designed to prepare you for the transition from seminary life to that of priestly ministry. For almost twenty years Leadership Roundtable has been working with pastors and other church leaders to equip them for the more temporal aspects of their ministerial roles. Many of the chapters selected for this current volume have been curated from volumes 1 and 2 of *A Pastor's Toolbox: Management Skills for Parish Leadership* (Liturgical Press, 2014, 2017). It also includes new chapters such as "Transition and Collaboration," "Intergenerational Ministry," "Collaboration and Co-Responsibility: The Heart of a Servant—Leading Like Jesus," and "Recruiting and Managing Volunteers."

It is our hope that this collection of leadership topics will inform and equip you to be the spiritual, inspirational, and competent leader the people entrusted to your care require of you.

We at Leadership Roundtable wish to thank our many experts whose wisdom is contained within this book and entrust them and all who read this to the intercession of St. John Vianney.

Transition and Collaboration

Tony Pogorelc

Every seminarian imagines the day when he will look at the seminary through the rearview mirror of his car for the final time as a seminarian. Like a bird leaving the nest, he wants to spread his wings and commence full-time parish ministry. Just as the mother bird passes on necessary codes for the fledgling to internalize, the seminary—a word that means a nursery in which seeds grow—does the same. It provides resources to be internalized to prepare the novice priest to begin his pastoral service to the people of God.

This chapter is on the transition from the seminary into a new "collaboration" stage: a word that means bringing to fruition together. Ecclesial ministry is not an individual project, it is the work of the church. Each member of a parish team brings his or her own charisms to ministry. To collaborate, one must know one's gifts and limitations and freely contribute them for the common good.

You began filling your toolbox for ministry in seminary with tools that have a valuable and indispensable foundation. Your toolbox may be organized according to the four dimensions of formation: human, spiritual, intellectual, and pastoral. These four dimensions shape both initial and ongoing formation. You are responsible for continuing your formation in all four of these disciplines.

Gifts from the Seminary

As a seminarian, you have had the opportunity to work collaboratively and build supportive and challenging relationships through ongoing dialogue with advisors, spiritual directors, pastoral supervisors, and peers. The same characteristics that enabled you to build fruitful relationships in the past will be valuable to build the relationships you need for your transition to the next stage of your ministry and life.

You can understand what it means to be a steward who is responsible and accountable. Remember the annual assessments you received of your capacity to be a good steward: What stands out for you from your evaluations as a collaborator? Were you the guy who had to be in charge or who would "go along to get along" and withhold your own perspective? Are you now someone who can contribute and receive input in a collaborative process?

It is important to take stock of the changes that occurred in you through formation. How is the man who glanced at the seminary through the rearview mirror different from the one who first saw it through the windshield? The freedom that comes from having completed seminary and being ordained places you in a privileged location to assess who God is calling you to become in this next phase of the journey: full-time ministry.

All ministry to the people of God begins with prayer and sustains you as a living witness to the people you serve. The seminary provided you with a structure for regular personal and communal prayer. As you enter the life of full-time pastoral ministry, you are going to need your own structure for liturgical and personal prayer. The Liturgy of the Hours, which was prayed communally in the seminary, becomes an individual prayer. Many priests find other demands competing with this prayerful consecration of one's day. One way to pray consistently is to structure two prayer periods into your day: one in the morning and one in the later part of the day. For morning people, the Office of Readings, Morning Prayer, and Daytime Prayer can begin the day, and Evening Prayer and Compline can conclude it. Non-morning people may want to pray more of the Hours later in the day. The most important thing is to continuously pray. You cannot collaborate with others to promote their spiritual growth without cultivating your own.

Likewise, you cannot credibly preach if you are not immersed in the Scriptures. By praying, reading commentaries, and through dialogue with others, you will grow in your capacity to integrate the Scriptures: the Law, the Prophets, the Wisdom literature, the Psalms, the Epistles, and the Gospels so that your preaching is rooted in them and is an expression of how they have converted you as a priest of Jesus Christ. Initial formation flows into ongoing formation, which is a process of growing in the image of Christ by conforming your actions to his as teacher and shepherd.

One way of doing this in a collaborative way is not to privatize your homily preparation. It is valuable to collaborate with your fellow preachers, who may be the pastor, your classmates, or priests and deacons in your area, as you discern what to preach about. It is also important to get critical feedback from those listening to your homilies. Know your congregation. What is the context of life in this parish? What are people going through? The best way to learn is to ask them. In some places, the structures are set up for doing so. In others, you need to figure out how you can do this. Building rapport with the staff, lay ministers, catechists, and teachers is good. This starts with showing respect to them. They all have something to teach you, and your life will be much easier and more effective if you realize this from the get-go. Putting this into practice may take time, so be patient.

Some seminarians treat spiritual direction as a hoop to jump through. In ministry, you learn its necessity, and you can embrace it or run away from it. So much of ministry is focused on serving others. You need to listen to them, remember them, respond to their needs and relativize your own. Ministry is about expending yourself. These demands can lead you to lose your life in Christ or to merely get lost. Spiritual direction has an important role in determining which it will be. I remember a priest reflecting that he loved to go to spiritual direction because it was one of the only times when the focus was on him, what nourished his prayer, his development, his feelings, and his needs.

As a priest, you can choose your spiritual director, and I think it is a good idea to go outside your diocesan system. You don't want to find out that your great spiritual director has been appointed the priest personnel director for your diocese. There is a good reason for a clear distinction between internal and external forums. Religious, both men and women, can be good spiritual directors for priests. There are also lay men and women who are formed in theology and spirituality, and that can make them excellent candidates to be spiritual directors for priests. As the sociologist Max Weber said: "You don't have to be Caesar to understand Caesar." You are looking for a good match, and for someone you respect and trust so you can be transparent.

Replanting the Dimensions of Formation

Human development is an important part of ongoing formation. How do you live a balanced life that allows for nourishing food and drink, exercise, relaxation, and healthy friendships? There are many resources to help you in this pursuit. Some institutions focus on priestly wellness. They all have an online presence. Take advantage of them. The more comfortable you are in your own skin, the more you can collaborate. Suppose you do not continue to develop a sense of who you are and are called to become. In that case, you will be stymied as you strive to enter into ministerial and authentic personal relationships.

Friendships with fellow priests are important. For most people, the number of close friends is few. This is also true for priests. There are different circles of friendship and they can support you in different ways. Don't be afraid to reach out to expand your circle of friends. It is a temptation to stick with people of your own age group, ethnicity, and ecclesial and social perspective. The theology of the priesthood calls priests to collaborate with the bishop and their fellow priests. The first step is getting to know them. Intergenerational friendships can be a blessing for those engaged in them and for the church. You can learn much about lived church history by reaching out to your elders. This can be a unity builder, because even if you might see things differently—and this is likely because you are from different generations—you will get a better sense of why.

Relationships with non-Catholic faith leaders can also enrich your ministry. We live in a pluralistic world, and that will not change even if someone wants to live in a silo. If you embrace the Second Vatican Council's vision that the church has a ministry to the world, collaboration with other Christian ministers and those of other religions will facilitate that mission. Popes St. John Paul II, Benedict, and Francis all testify to this.

Likewise, intellectual development must be an ongoing pursuit. To have something worthwhile to say, you must be feeding your mind. Read books. Perhaps you might become part of a book discussion club. Online and social media sources are not enough for today's priests. You also need to know how to assess the quality of the literature and media you consume. Claims need to be backed up with data. If you are unsure that something is true, do not repeat it. As Pope Francis cautions in his encyclical *Fratelli Tutti*: "Dialogue is often confused with something quite different: the feverish exchange of opinions on social networks, frequently based on media information that is not always reliable. These exchanges are merely parallel monologues" (200).[1]

Calumny is making false and defamatory statements about someone in order to damage their reputation. The *Catechism of the Catholic Church* says it "offend[s] against the virtues of justice and charity" (2479).[2] Avoid being pressured into speaking when you do not think it is prudent. As the wise saying goes: "It is better to be silent and thought a fool than to open your mouth and remove all doubt." Don't be a priest who embarrasses the church. It is necessary to continue to collaborate in intellectual growth. Talk to people with different perspectives, not to point out their faults, but to understand and learn from them.

The Mission

Ordination sends a person forth. You are commissioned. Ongoing discernment, reflection, and dialogue will help you to develop a sense of what you are there to do. You need to identify and articulate your orientation toward the people of God. How do you see them? You also need to identify and articulate what you bring to the table. The seminary should have given you a sense of your gifts and limits. Self-knowledge should give you confidence in your self-presentation. Do you trust yourself to succeed? What does transparency require? What is it helpful for people to know about you? What you reveal should be for the good of the ministry. You must discern the things that are appropriate to share and those that are not. Things that you are working out personally and spiritually belong to conversations with your spiritual director or your mentor or your closest confidants.

When you join a parish team, you are becoming part of a system that has a history. It existed before you, and it will persist after you are gone. Your task is to come to know it. Who are the individuals you work with? What is their history? What are their gifts and limits? You must also get to know the relationships between and among those who make the team an entity greater than the sum of its parts. You can do this by observation and drawing on your intuition. Describe your impressions to your mentor or other experienced persons you trust.

Effective communication will be important. The parish will be a diverse audience and may offer an experience far different from those you have had as a seminarian. You need to get to know your parishioners. It's not a one-size-fits-all operation; parish cultures vary. How do you best communicate? Verbal and nonverbal communication are important. People won't remember everything you say, but they will remember how you make them feel. They know when you are taking them seriously and showing them respect. Nonverbal communication is especially important regarding this. To know people, you must listen to them and remember them and what they say. *Fratelli Tutti* suggests that dialogue is "[a]pproaching, speaking, listening, looking at, coming to know and understand one another, and to find common ground" (198). Again, you need to seriously reflect and dialogue about how to best do this for yourself in your particular context.

Your relationship with your immediate supervisor, your pastor, is an important one. Throughout our lives we have been exposed to different pastors. We know they are not all the same and that we have appreciated some more than others. It is important to understand and accept who your current pastor is. One of the first things to do is to assess the situation. Get to know about your pastor's previous experience. Is he a lifelong Catholic? Where did he go to seminary? What are his theological and spiritual orientations? This is an important first step for understanding him and where he is coming from. Is pastoring this parish his full-time job? That will greatly determine his availability and very likely influence what you will be asked to do. Being half-time in the chancery or some other specialized ministry is a lot different than being a full-time pastor. What are his gifts and what are his limitations? Every human being has both, and being aware of them will help you to work with him as well as help you to discover how you can work most effectively in the parish.

It will be important for you to discern how to communicate with your pastor most effectively. Does he like the straightforward approach or one that is more gentle or indirect? Is he someone who doesn't like to be put on the spot? I had a pastor whom I found with certain matters it was best to leave a note. If he wanted to take up the issue, he would, and if not, I would not hear from him. Rather than catering to the quixotic needs of the pastor, I think better advice is to determine best practices and suggest them to the pastor. It is also important, if your pastor is an international priest, to have a sense of the communication in his culture. There are books and other resources to help you with this kind of learning.

As you get to know him, you will discover if he is a mentor who can meet your needs, or if you need to seek additional advice and mentorship elsewhere. It is important for you to be aware of the experienced priests who can help you grow into the priestly role. You don't have to have just one. Building a network is most valuable. Self-reflection is important here. It is important to identify and clarify what type of mentorship and advice you need. No matter what, you cannot leave the pastor out of the picture.

Identify what you are looking for from him, and to what extent he can provide this, and appropriately communicate with him. Then determine what supplementary resources you need. Recall the tools from the seminary that may help you to navigate this situation. The bottom line is that, for this assignment to succeed, you have a responsibility to learn how to work with your pastor effectively.

In some parishes there are clear job descriptions, and in others there are not. You need to determine if there are or are not such job descriptions in place. This is about boundaries: What is your turf, and what is not? If there is not a clear definition of responsibilities, it would be prudent to see if you can get one. Boundaries may be formal or informal. Developing a working job description will involve the pastor and can involve other members of the parish team and staff. Ideally, you will be assessed according to the job description that is established. Even if it is not officially written, you can write it down and present it to the relevant parties as a memorandum of understanding. Be conscious of their reception and document it.

In the parish, identify those who seem most willing to work with you and want to help you to develop and succeed. Assess if the environment lends itself to cooperation or if is it siloed. What is the level of freedom to ask questions and consult others? Identify the formal and informal leaders and who dominates. What is the particular expertise of the pastor, the team, and the staff? Who is the best person to consult when facing a particular type of issue?

There is asceticism in collaboration; it can require self-sacrifice, but it is worth doing. Sometimes you will have to be the proactive one and reach out. Indeed, you may think, "I'm the new guy and the veterans should have set this up." That may be true, but those sentiments may just reinforce the status quo. Your orientation needs to be about how you can embrace your responsibility to effectively work with this pastor, team, and staff. You need to ask yourself: Does the communication or action I am contemplating strengthen our working collaboration and help us work effectively, or does it set up obstacles? You may need to sacrifice your ego frequently.

Integration is a process that occurs over time. You are laying a foundation for your life and ministry as a priest. Focus on the four dimensions (human, spiritual, intellectual, and pastoral). The better you integrate these dimensions, the healthier and happier you will be. You need to identify your needs and continuously discern how best to meet them. These needs will change with the passage of time and changing circumstances, and you will want to be all the more attentive during periods of heightened stress. The more wholeness and holiness you develop, the better collaborator you will be, because you will bring the genuine gifts God has given you to the table. This mode of service will enable you to be a credible and faithful presider at the table of Word and Sacrament.

Endnotes

1. Pope Francis, *Fratelli Tutti*, On Fraternity and Social Friendship (October 3, 2020).

2. *Catechism of the Catholic Church*, 2nd ed. (United States Catholic Conference—Libreria Editrice Vaticana, 1997).

Developing a Vision

Dominic Perri

Proverbs 29 tells us, "Where there is no vision, the people perish" (v. 18, King James Version). I wouldn't say that most parishes today are on the verge of extinction. What I would suggest, though, is that they are hungry for vision. What exactly do I mean by vision, and how is it different from mission? If you've asked that question yourself and are lost for an answer, you're not alone. I hear it all the time.

Very simply, your mission is a statement of identity. As seminarians you are each preparing to one day be a leader in a parish community, a pastor. Mission is something of which you will need to be very aware. It's who you are as a parish, or any other type of ministry. We are, for example, the Parish of St. Mary's. And we exist to preach and teach the sacraments and bring the Gospel to those in our community. As a statement of identity, it generally does not change, nor should it change, at least for decades. To relate this to the for-profit world, take a company like Nike. It's a shoe seller and provider of athletic goods. That's not likely going to change from one year to the next. It's a fundamental statement of their corporate identity.

Vision, on the other hand, is where you want to go in the future. It's the ability to say, "We're at point A and want to get to point B." It's where you're trying to lead people. Vision is what I call a *desired future*. To personalize that a bit, I'm the son of Italian immigrants who grew up in Louisville, Kentucky, of all places. That's my identity. I can't change that. But my vision of where I wanted to go has changed over my life. I was determined to go to college, so I enrolled in The Catholic University of America. After graduation, I wanted to leave my mark in the workplace, then get married and start a family. My vision involved setting goals for myself, moving toward them, and setting new goals. Unlike mission, your vision changes over time.

How many of you have had people come up and ask, "What's your vision for the parish?" As pastors, your vision is to lead your people. But where do you want to take them? That's where your vision is crucial. The faithful are basically asking, "Where do you see yourself taking us?" It seems very simple. We start at point A, and go to point B. That's what vision is. That's what leading is.

But it's not as simple as it appears. Anyone who's ever been part of drafting a vision statement for an organization knows what I'm talking about. Too often, what ultimately gets produced is tacked on the wall like the Declaration of Independence; it looks very pretty, but that's essentially the end of the story. The process is often difficult and wrenching, and the toughest part is afterward when people say, "I don't know what we got out of this. I don't know how it changed our organization." So, what I want to really focus on is helping you think about and create a vision that will allow you to move your parish to where you want it to be. And hopefully without the pain and aggravation I'm sure many of you have experienced.

Knowing What Road to Take

Why is vision so important? There's no better instructor here than Lewis Carroll, who, in *Alice in Wonderland*, describes a scene where Alice encounters the Cheshire Cat. As many of you will recall, Alice asks for directions: "Would you tell me, please, which way I ought to go from here?" The Cheshire Cat replies, "That depends a good deal on where you want to get to." When Alice says she doesn't really know where she wants to go, the Cat famously replies, "Then it doesn't matter which way you go."[1]

The message is clear: If you don't know where you want to go, then you drift. And as I've seen through my experiences with parishes around the US, there are many in various stages of drift. They're in maintenance mode. It's akin to treading water. And this, unfortunately, leads to a bit of a leadership and vision vacuum, so that when well-intentioned folks in the parish show up with a bright and shiny idea, the feeling is, "Maybe we should pursue it. Since we don't know where we're going, any road will get us there." It's the polar opposite of having a vision that allows you to say, "This is where we're going, or not going." With respect to the latter, it might be a great program. It may have worked well in another parish. You may be very excited about it. But with vision as your guide, you may also realize that it's not appropriate for your parish. Just as importantly, though, your vision allows you to refocus, to move decisively in a new direction.

To give you another perspective: George Wilson, a friend and mentor of mine, is a Jesuit who did organization-development work with church groups for more than thirty years. He has stated that many church organizations don't have a resource problem; they have a *vison* problem. It's no secret that many Catholic parishes and organizations spend a lot of time lamenting how strapped they are for funds and how hard it is to attract competent people to their ranks. But that's hardly the end of the discussion. I believe we have to ask ourselves a very fundamental question: Are we putting out a product with a compelling enough vision to attract people and resources? In the end, people want to be part of something that's going somewhere, and if it appears we're just treading water, that we're in perpetual maintenance mode, then they're going to turn away from the church in droves.

What, then, should our vision be? How do we get people enthused about our "product"? Our lofty vision for our parish is typically to bring all souls to Jesus. The problem is that it doesn't necessarily give you a direction for where you want to be tomorrow or next month or next year. In other words, it doesn't give you a vision—a desired future—that can help you plan and make decisions for your parish.

Here's an example from the secular world that may help. Consider film directors. They must have a very clear sense of what their final product is going to look like, even if it hasn't been created yet. They have a *desired future*. This is the kind of product we want. Think of yourselves as directors creating a film. You may be shooting seven scenes in three cities—let's say Los Angeles, Chicago, and Newark. But if scenes one and five are in Los Angeles, you don't go to Los Angeles for scene one, then the other cities for scenes two, three, and four, only to return to Los Angeles for scene five. That wouldn't make any sense. You shoot scenes one and five in Los Angeles in tandem. The point is, directors must have in mind what the final product is going to look like in order to pull off that kind of logistical exercise. Since it's not happening in sequence, they need to see the bigger picture through the smaller component parts in each city. Indeed, if you listen to interviews with directors, they will invariably say, "I knew what each scene had to deliver because I had the bigger picture of how they would all fit together in the end."

The question I pose to you as future pastors and leaders in your parishes is this: Do you have a vision of what you want your parish to look like in three years? Can you look at the smaller parts of that mosaic right now and say, "They have to be this way because here is what the final product will look like"? That's the idea of vision. That's the idea of desired future.

Another example from the secular world is Apple. When the computer-maker was founded, its vision was to get computers into the hands of everyday people, to make the devices accessible to every home. And the company succeeded beyond its wildest dreams. It had a vision of where it wanted to be. Its iconic leader, the late Steve Jobs, reinforced the point. After starting the company, he left, and returned when it almost went under in the mid-1990s. At that moment, Apple had roughly eighty-five products. Jobs drew a two-by-two matrix and said, "We're going to have four products—a desktop for home, a desktop for business, a laptop for home, and a laptop for business. We're getting rid of everything else." Not surprisingly, that sent a few shock waves through the organization. But that was the point at which Apple began to turn around and become the juggernaut it is today. Jobs had a very clear vision about where he wanted to take the company, and within a given time frame. He saw the future he wanted. And that's a powerful lesson for the church as well.

How a Vision Can Change

Let me give you an example that hits closer to home. My own parish—Old Saint Patrick's in downtown Chicago—dates back to the 1850s. By the early 1980s, it was on the verge of closing, a victim of the construction of the interstate highway system that tore apart neighborhoods and forced residents to flee. When Fr. Jack Wall took over as pastor in 1983, four members remained in the entire parish.

That would have sounded the death knell for most organizations, but Jack walked in and said, "I've got a vision for this parish. But it won't be like most parishes that are focused on attracting families and children. After all, we're in downtown Chicago, where nobody really lives. So, we're going to become a place for young adults. Downtown Chicago is filled with young, single Catholic professionals who are coming to the city every day, and we can serve them in a host of ways—with programs at their lunch breaks and programs after work. We can tailor programs to them because they're now going to parishes in the suburbs, which are focused on families, and that's not who they are."

Jack had a bold vision, a desired future, for his parish. In some cases, that meant telling people, "We're not going to do this because it doesn't advance our vision." And in short order, amazing things began to happen. Young adults flocked there. One of the reasons was that Old Saint Pat's offered a Saturday night block party where people could come to eat, listen to bands, and mingle. I should note that these block parties raised money for the parish's social outreach program, so they were connected to the mission. Interestingly, what also happened at those block parties was that lots of young, single Catholic professionals started meeting each other, getting married, and having families.

And by 1989, when waves of Catholic parishes were closing their schools, Old Saint Pat's was just opening theirs. Today, it serves the needs of four thousand registered families from over sixty zip codes. And Jack will tell you that lots of people in those early years came to him and said, "How can you not have X, Y, Z—the standard way a parish serves families?" His answer was simple and direct: "That's not the future we're trying to get to."

There's no question your vision will change. It did for Apple and it did for Old Saint Pat's, once they started to grow and discovered they had different needs. Where it starts, though, is looking around and asking yourself, "Where are we now, and what will someone who shows up for Sunday Mass at our parish three years from now experience that's different?" Are you able to paint that picture? Can you talk about the desired future as the fulfillment of what you want your parish to become?

Vision brings that desired future into focus. And the other nice thing is that gifts and resources often follow in its wake. Just look at Old Saint Pat's. Each year its annual block party—now held on Friday *and* Saturday nights—attracts thousands of young people and raises several hundred thousand dollars. These contributions are then used to fund the church's social-outreach programs. I'm not suggesting you come to the conclusion, "Oh my gosh, how do I ever come up with something like that?" What I am suggesting, though, is that when your vision, your desired future, is compelling enough, people and resources will inevitably follow.

Charting Your Course as a Parish

A clear vision also allows you to say *no* to certain things. And that's absolutely crucial. In your lives as pastors, no doubt people will come up to you and say, "Father, I've got a great idea for our parish." Or, "I just came back from this retreat and witnessed a program we have to have immediately." What's the measuring stick that allows you to say yes or no to each well-intentioned idea? Is it how much energy you have at the moment, or whether or not they caught you at the right time of the day? Absolutely not. Having a window into the future and being able to say to a member of your parish, "I appreciate your idea, but it doesn't quite line up with where we want this parish to be in another three years," should be your measuring stick.

Determining what you want your parish to become, of course, is no easy task. It means spending considerable time thinking about the needs of the people around you. What's unique about who we are as a parish? What's our history? How is the community changing? Setting a direction for the future means listening—to your staff, especially those who have been there the longest, to your parish council, to your parishioners, and to the community at large. You also need to study the demographic data. It may show, for example, that you're in an area where Hispanics are the fastest-growing population segment, prompting you to say, "We need to become a one hundred percent bicultural and bilingual English-Spanish parish. That's our desired future." What, then, will people experience when they come to our parish in another three years? Well, they'll see how we've managed to smoothly integrate the two cultures. There will be bilingual liturgies, bulletins in both English and Spanish, and active community outreach. And to get to that goal, we're going to start right now to build intercultural awareness through events, programs, and trips. That's how we plan to make our vision real.

Here's another example of what I mean by vision. In the course of listening and talking to others, you might come to see there's a hunger for a fuller expression of Catholic teachings on social justice. Therefore, your vision might be to convey that theme through parish preaching, or visits to local soup kitchens, or through faith-sharing groups where members reflect on how to embed Catholic social teachings in their everyday lives. That's the kind of experience you might want to build for parishioners, and your vision is the vehicle that will get you there.

There will always be folks who say, "No, no, Father. I don't think we should do it that way." And there's nothing preventing you from saying to them, "Here are my initial thoughts. Let's now take them to the parish council for its feedback." You can, and should, consult with others. At Old Saint Pat's, for example, we held a summit where we brought in seventy-five parish leaders for a day-and-a-half meeting to get input. At the end of the day, though, you will be the leader of the parish and have to be able to say, "Based on what I've seen and heard, here is the direction in which we need to be moving. Here is where the Holy Spirit is beckoning us. Let's embark on this vision together."

One Church's Response

Church of the Nativity, a parish in the town of Timonium, Maryland, developed a very distinct vision of its desired future. Members looked around and realized they were in a sleepy northern suburb of Baltimore where the church really didn't matter in the lives of many people. So they began asking themselves some key questions: What experience do we want people to have when they come here on the weekend? How do we transform that personal experience from just sitting in a pew for forty-five minutes to actually becoming a disciple—to getting involved in a ministry, joining a small discussion group, or playing a role in community outreach? And, if we become a church filled with disciples, what activities need to occur throughout the week?

As members detailed in a book they eventually wrote about their journey called *Rebuilt*, they decided to concentrate on creating a dynamic, irresistible weekend experience. It featured programs for children and students, lots of music, and meaningful messages crafted by the church's ministers. In other words, they created the kind of engaging, energetic environment that would encourage newcomers to return, and regular members to become even more active. To get to that level, though, they realized they'd have to really do their homework, planning the program and events for each Saturday and Sunday weeks or even months in advance. They'd have to review the Scriptures and decide on which lessons or themes to dwell. And they'd have to thoughtfully integrate them with the weekend's music and hospitality.

In the course of saying yes to those ideas that would advance their vision, the parish also had the foresight—and strength—to say no to ideas that wouldn't. Bingo was one of those. So were Catholic Youth Organization (CYO) and sports. And to those people who objected to their choices, parish leaders politely suggested that this church might not be the right place for them and guided them elsewhere.

Vision Takes Time and Patience

How do you know when you've arrived at a vision that can really energize your parish? Here's a simple yardstick: when you share your vision with people and they get excited about it. When they say, "Father, we want to be part of that," or "This is something we can buy into."

Be aware that developing the right vision for your parish may take some time. If you want a fully formed blueprint that fills your leaders with an unquenchable fire, one that really inspires people, it must be part of a deliberative, thoughtful, unhurried process. It must involve constant back-and-forth with those around you. In the course of that conversation you might learn, for example, there's a discernible desire to become a parish that lives and breathes the message of Pope Francis. Or to become a parish where young people feel especially welcome. Or a parish where *all* generations feel welcome. The core question then becomes, What do we need to do, or stop doing, to get us there?

Most importantly, don't be discouraged or get sidetracked as you embark on this timely journey. As the leader of your congregation, continue to reflect on it and pray on it as you provoke a spirited discussion with the faithful. Stay focused and committed. Only then will a collective vision emerge with the energy to take your parish in a bold and exciting new direction, a desired future.

To paraphrase Proverbs 29, where there *is* a vision, the people flourish!

Endnote

1. Lewis Carroll, *Alice in Wonderland* (New York: Scholastic, 2001), 74.

Collaboration and Co-Responsibility: The Heart of a Servant—Leading Like Jesus

Jeffry Odell Korgen and Cesar Izqierdo

Imagine you are one of Christ's apostles, sharing the Passover meal with Jesus prior to his Passion. You feel excitement in the room but also tension. During supper, Jesus rises from the table, takes off his outer robe, and ties a towel around his waist. He pours water into a basin and begins to wash the feet of his apostles. What does it feel like when he reaches you? Your teacher kneels before you, washing your dusty feet.

When Jesus reaches Simon Peter, Peter asks, "Lord, are you going to wash my feet?" Jesus replies, "You do not know now what I am doing, but later you will understand." Peter responds, "You will never wash my feet." But Jesus will have none of this: "Unless I wash you, you have no share with me." Later, he adds, "Do you know what I have done to you? You call me Teacher and Lord—and you are right, for that is what I am. So if I, your Lord and Teacher, have washed your feet, you also ought to wash one another's feet. For I have set you an example, that you also should do as I have done to you" (John 13:6-15).

Jesus has spoken like this before. You recall: "Whoever wants to be first must be last of all and servant of all" (Mark 9:35) and "[T]he greatest among you must become like the . . . one who serves" (Luke 22:26). You realize now, Christ has taught you how to lead his church through this simple action of foot washing.

The answers to our deepest questions about church leadership are in this meditation. In the pages that follow, we will unpack how Christ's model of servant leadership will help you become a better church leader, one who leads like Jesus—a "servant-leader." We will illuminate the *specific behaviors* that will help you to become a servant-leader and stronger disciple of Christ. While we have based this servant leadership model on Christ's teaching and example, we also draw from the Hebrew Scriptures and the lives of the saints. Examples from parish life will also help illustrate the servant-leader behaviors.

What Is a Servant-Leader?

A Catholic servant-leader is motivated by the desire to serve and develops other disciples of Christ to accomplish the church's mission together. Influenced by the writings of Catholic scholars like Dan Ebener and secular writers like Robert Greenleaf, we believe that Catholic servant-leaders share the following seven key qualities:

1. Utilizes Relational Approaches to Invitation,
2. Cultivates Spirituality,
3. Shows Concern for Ministry Team Members,
4. Practices Empowerment,
5. Demonstrates Humility,
6. Models Visionary Discipleship, and
7. Embraces the Preferential Option for the Poor.

We explore the specific behaviors among servant-leaders that illustrate these qualities in the sections that follow.

A Servant-Leader *Utilizes Relational Approaches to Invitation*

Think about it. Did Jesus build his movement by putting notices in the *Fisherman's Bulletin*? Of course not! Nor does a servant-leader. Servant-leaders grow the church by leading like Jesus, eating and drinking with sinners, getting acquainted with their dreams, skills, and fears. Christ invited sinners into discipleship, calling, "Follow me" and "Come and see." In the parish, a servant-leader does not rely on pulpit announcements or the parish bulletin to attract disciples. They *lead like Jesus*, sharing fellowship with and listening to the people of God. Once they understand the skills, dreams, and capacities of potential team members, servant-leaders invite them into specific ministries.

As a new parish youth minister in the Bible Belt of southwest Missouri, I (Jeff) held listening sessions with my youth group. They surprised me with the lament, "Our friends tell us that the Bible says we're going to hell because we're Catholic! We want to learn more about Scripture so we can fight back!" In thinking through a response, I thought of a couple in the parish who were very active in Little Rock Scripture Study. I sensed they wanted to connect with young people, and they clearly had a love of the Word of God. So, I invited them to lead a youth Bible study. I was not trying to "fill a slot." I matched two needs for spiritual growth—the teens' desire to learn more about the Bible and the couple's wish to bring their own study of Scripture to a new level. Their unspoken desire to connect with youth made it a perfect match—and it was!

This dimension of servant leadership begins with "eating and drinking with sinners," though the eating and drinking is optional—you can simply set up a half-hour meeting to get to know a disciple's interests, passions, skills, and relationships. In time, you will begin to discern what *part* of the Body of Christ this person is or can become. Inviting them into a ministry, assigning a specific role, and providing coaching to help them grow from their experiences in ministry are the next steps. Helping people learn from success and failure in ministry is also essential to authentic and effective servant leadership.

A Servant-Leader *Cultivates Spirituality*

Servant-leaders know that everything they achieve in ministry comes from God and work to cultivate both their own spirituality and that of parish staff and volunteers. They develop a mature understanding of God and use Christian ethics to make decisions. When conflict arises, they resolve it in a manner consistent with Christian discipleship. Situations with no easy answers evoke listening, prayer, and discernment.

A servant-leader also helps a team ground their ministry in spirituality. Many of us have volunteered or worked in a parish where the spirit of "getting things done" has replaced a grounding in the Holy Spirit. But consider all the times Jesus went away to pray, leaving behind the ministries of teaching and healing—sometimes for as long as forty days (e.g., Luke 4:1-15, 5:16, 6:12-13, 22:39-44). Becoming a servant-leader is not something to *do*; it is something to *be*. Cultivating a strong Christian spirituality is essential to building that identity.

It's said that *we can't give what we don't have.* I (Fr. Cesar) have come to realize this as a newly ordained priest assigned to a parish that runs activities and events 24/7. In the face of a prevailing attitude of "getting things done" we learned to incorporate prayer throughout our daily parish life. If we know that all our ministries are interconnected with the Eucharist, "the source and summit of the Christian life" (*Catechism of the Catholic Church* 1324; quoting *Lumen Gentium* 11), we must direct all that we do to make that reality part of our lives.

For us, the Liturgy of the Hours has facilitated prayer for both staff and volunteers. This period of prayer—whether offered at the church, the parish office, or the school—has made an important difference. We have committed to pray Morning Prayer with the teachers before classes begin, to pray the Office of Readings with the deacons before morning Mass, and to have Midday Prayer with the staff before lunch. Having prayer as an integral part of our ministries has given all of us the attitude and capacity to face conflicts in a Christian manner. Situations with no easy answers evoke listening, prayer, and discernment. When we are in communion with each other through prayer, we all grow and find the real meaning of our ministries.

A Servant-Leader *Shows Concern for Ministry Team Members*

In his groundbreaking essay "The Servant as Leader," Robert K. Greenleaf shared the results of his research on effective management styles: the most successful leaders, whether they led businesses, nonprofits, or educational institutions, were servant-leaders. One of the most frequent outcomes of servant leadership, he observed, was healthier employees. We see this quality in the Gospels, as Jesus forms the disciples—especially the twelve. Sometimes he encourages; sometimes he corrects. At times he issues challenges that are ignored; in other moments, people drop whatever they are doing and follow him. When his followers and their families are sick, Jesus heals them, even bringing Lazarus back from the dead. The disciples come alive through the encounter with the risen Christ, "hearts burning within" them.

Among parish leaders, physical, mental, and spiritual health problems are often expressions of stress. Does this ring true for you? Many of us put a lot of pressure on ourselves to control every aspect of our work. Sometimes we don't trust other people to take on meaningful and important roles. I (Jeff) once coached a parish director of Hispanic ministry named Yazmin who recognized this tendency in herself. Her need to do everything in this broad ministry was affecting her morale and health. She was burning out.

Moses had this problem too. After the Hebrews escaped from slavery, disputes among them erupted during the long journey to the Promised Land. Moses settled each dispute himself, teaching "the statutes and in- structions of God" (Exod 18:16). His father-in-law, Jethro, observed Moses at work and took him aside, explaining, "What you are doing is not good. You will surely wear yourself out, both you and these people with you. For the task is too heavy for you; you cannot do it alone" (Exod 18:17-18). Jethro offered an alternative—appointing judges, "men who fear God, are trustworthy, and hate dishonest gain" (Exod 18:21), who adjudicated the minor cases and left the most important conflicts for Moses himself. Moses followed Jethro's advice and became a better leader.

We love Jethro's observation, "You will surely wear yourself out, both you *and these people with you.*" It makes me think of Yazmin. I was, of course, concerned for her health, but I was also concerned about the health of the volunteer leaders on her ministry team. They were "worn out" by her leadership style too! Our coaching began to focus not only on the lessons of Moses and Jethro, but also on Jesus as a leader who develops leaders. We discussed how she might select the right leaders to develop, under- stand their stress levels, and help them manage difficult situations. She would continue to monitor their spiritual health and assist her volunteers in achieving ministry/life balance—all behaviors of servant-leaders.

As Yazmin considered the possibilities, her entire body began to change. She grew taller before my eyes, shoulders no longer stooped, face radiant. "I can do that!" she said. And she did, opening a new chapter of leadership in her life, much like Moses.

A Servant-Leader *Practices Empowerment*

But Yazmin's journey didn't end there. Servant-leaders don't just delegate, they share power and decision-making with others on their ministry teams. They assign important tasks to other team members, not just activities they prefer not to do themselves. Like Jesus, servant-leaders build meaningful relationships through which they learn both the capabilities of their team members and how they can challenge them to fulfill their potential as leaders.

Jesus utilized these skills when he selected and developed the twelve. When he created this special leadership group of men within his larger movement, he did not ask, "Are there any volunteers?" No, Christ called each of the apostles by name (Luke 6:12-16). In parishes, servant-leaders do the same, utilizing their relational skills to dig deeper—to understand the motivations and interests of each parish leader. By doing so, they invite the right people into positions of leadership.

The founder of the Catholic Worker movement and candidate for sainthood, Dorothy Day, practiced empowerment among leaders in her movement. In the early 1970s she invited nineteen-year-old college dropout Robert Ellsberg to become managing editor of the historic *Catholic Worker* newspaper. Day took the time to get to know the young man, what he was capable of, and and the kinds of challenges to which he could rise. He accepted the job and continued in it until Day's death and his return to higher education. He is now the publisher and editor-in-chief of Orbis Books, the publishing arm of the Maryknoll Fathers and Brothers. How did Day know she was meeting a future star in Catholic publishing? By leading like Jesus, asking a lot of questions of him during meals. This was her leadership-identification process within the Catholic Worker, surfacing leaders and assigning responsibilities based on an understanding of each person's unique strengths.

Within the parish context, servant-leaders also empower others by creating a culture in which people are not afraid of making mistakes. If everyone is afraid of disappointing Father—or whomever coordinates a ministry—they will not express the creativity necessary to bring the ministry to the next level. Servant-leaders are magnanimous towards team members who make mistakes, treating mistakes and failures as learning opportunities. I (Jeff) employed this approach as a parish youth minister, convening core teams of both youth and adult leaders to sort out "what went well" and "what could have gone better" following each meeting or event. By creating a culture where mistakes and failure were *expected* and seen as *learning opportunities*, they become positive experiences for a ministry team. It also promotes candor if the group discusses team leaders' mistakes. Believe me, I contributed plenty of material for my youth ministry team to discuss!

A Servant-Leader *Demonstrates Humility*

Related to empowerment is the quality of humility. A servant-leader has an acute sense that they are not God—they are servants to the mission of Christ and his church. Jesus tries to teach this message to the disciples throughout the Gospels, most notably in his rebuke of James and John (or was it their mother?) to sit at his left and right when he comes into his glory. The "Sons of Thunder" make this request in Mark 10 (Mom makes her play in Matthew 20), disappointing Jesus and causing an argument with the other ten apostles.

Jesus then calls the twelve together and says, "You know that among the Gentiles those whom they recognize as their rulers lord it over them, and their great ones are tyrants over them. But it is not so among you; but whoever wishes to become great among you must be your servant" (Mark 10:42-43). In Matthew's Gospel, he states, "Truly I tell you, unless you change and become like children, you will never enter the kingdom of heaven" (Matt 18:3). Children were among the most vulnerable people in society at the time. To become as simple as a child was risky.

This mind-set is at the heart of the servant-leader's practice of humility. Servant-leaders do not let power go to their heads. They are good listeners and accept criticism well. They are open to ideas that are not their own. They are nonjudgmental when relating to team members and tolerant of people's quirks and eccentricities.

In the parish, servant-leaders express these behaviors in how they interact with other team members. To be honest, this has been the hardest area for me (Jeff) to develop. In an argument with a colleague at the Diocese of Metuchen, where I served as executive director for diocesan planning, he blurted out, "You think you're better than everyone!" The reality was that I was insecure in my new position. I was a social minister, not a diocesan administrator! Truly, I felt less competent than others. But colleagues were beginning to see me as a know-it-all.

So, I started asking more questions and tried to integrate others' ideas into my own. When colleagues responded to my ideas with criticism, rather than react defensively, I asked them questions. I tried to see more of their gifts and less of their quirks. The situation improved, and I became more confident myself. Though I have a long way to go, I have recognized this as an issue and am more aware of the behaviors I need to focus on. Humility is one of the most important underlying qualities of servant leadership—and perhaps that is why Jesus speaks so much about it in the Gospels.

A Servant-Leader *Models Visionary Discipleship*

We noted earlier how important it is to focus on the church's mission rather than dwelling on one's own wants, needs, and leadership aims. Jesus again provides us with a model, maintaining his commitment to the Father's vision despite extreme temptations in the Judean desert (Luke 4:1-13; Matt 4:1-11). Later, he rebukes Peter when Peter suggests that it is not necessary that Jesus undergo his Passion (Matt 16:23). Christ stays focused on his mission even when key leaders in his movement suggest an easier path.

A parish servant-leader keeps this focus as well and expresses it in a way that team members, and indeed the whole parish, can understand. In the words of the prophet Habakkuk, "Make it plain" (Hab 2:2-3). In the parish, this approach conveys a sense of purpose to parishioners, and it becomes easier to draw them together around a common goal. Moreover, a servant-leader helps the group *act* on the vision, making it concrete through specific actions and results.

When Fr. Michael White and lay associate Tom Corcoran grew tired of the decline in membership and spirit at Church of the Nativity in Timonium, Maryland, in the 2010s, they embarked on a cycle of renewal focused on making disciples of "the lost" and helping them, in turn, make other disciples. While implementing that vision, they focused on enhancing parishioners' weekend experience and drawing more men into discipleship. Not everyone in the parish was excited about these new directions, and as outreach to the unchurched began, one-third of the community deserted the parish. While this was a discouraging consequence, White and Corcoran remained committed to their mission. Within two years, hundreds of new parishioners began to attend, pushing the community out of its own church at Christmas and Easter into public spaces. Church of the Nativity's journey is described in the award-winning 2013 book *Rebuilt*, and the community now shares its parish-renewal model through the organization Rebuilt Parish.

A Servant-Leader *Embraces the Preferential Option for the Poor*

A servant-leader keeps the vision of making disciples at the forefront, but also remembers Christ's description of the Last Judgment in Matthew (25:31-46). The Lord's words, "I was hungry, and you gave me food," will be familiar to most readers. In this parable, Jesus identifies *himself* with poor and vulnerable people. How we treat the poor, Christ describes, is how we treat the Lord himself.

Within a parish, this concept manifests itself *externally* through social ministries for charity and justice, but also *internally* through how we engage those parishioners who have the weakest voices, whose opinions may not be taken seriously by many parishioners. Maybe it's because of their race, age, sex, disability, culture, or simply because they are introverted. There are many reasons people are overlooked in parishes. A servant-leader notices who is participating and who isn't, encouraging people less likely to contribute in meetings to speak up and bringing up the perspectives of those not present. Externally, a servant-leader shows concern for people living in economic poverty and other vulnerable persons (e.g., the unborn, elderly, people with disabilities, and people with addictions). They speak up for those without a voice in society and help people speak up for themselves.

The late bishop of Saginaw, Michigan, Kenneth Untener, once decreed that diocesan parishes would ask a single question for six months during *every* parish meeting: "What does this have to do with the poor?" Such an inquiry made space for new conversations within the parish in a way that did not prescribe specific activities—it simply fostered conversation. Consider the various activities in your parish. What would happen if you asked this question?

Becoming a Servant-Leader

To some degree, many of us are already on our way to becoming servant-leaders because we come to church with the desire to serve. But take a moment to review the behaviors noted in each of the preceding seven sections. Rate yourself on a scale from 1 to 10 for each of the seven categories. Then review the scores. Which is highest? Which is lowest? Which behaviors would be most important for you to adopt right now? Which would be important to adopt over the long haul?

It might appear that becoming a servant-leader is simply a matter of reflecting on the teaching and example of Christ, as noted in the preceding pages. Reflection and prayer on the notion of servant leadership and its roots in Scripture and church teaching are indeed important. But just as you can think your way into a new way of acting, you can also act your way into a new way of thinking. Try simply adopting some of the behaviors listed in this chapter and notice how it affects your mind-set.

People on your ministry teams will begin to respond to you differently. You will find yourself becoming a stronger disciple and leader, one who washes the feet of other disciples by adopting these servant-leader behaviors. "For I have set you an example, that you also should do as I have done to you" (John 13:15).

4

Intercultural Competencies for Ministry

Allan Figueroa Deck

For a book purporting to be a "toolbox," that is, a practical resource for engaging complex challenges with handy and accessible aids for remedying the situation, this chapter may seem at first rather theoretical. All I can say is that I am a big believer in what some wise person said long ago: "Nothing is more practical than a *good* theory." Intercultural competence needs to be addressed from a more penetrating and comprehensive theoretical *and* practical perspective because what is at stake, really, is a deeper grasp of the Catholic Church's very identity and mission, one that goes beyond mere pragmatism. It is about what we do, but also about what we become and are! The reality of globalization, migrations, commerce, communications, and the struggle for human dignity has implications for the most basic units of the Christian community today—for each Christian individually as well as for the family, parish, diocese, apostolic movement, school, or Catholic organization. Hence mind-sets, heart-sets, and skill-sets in intercultural encounter have become increasingly indispensable for life, work, and ministry in today's world and church. Both domestically and globally, matters of war and peace, communications, travel, migration, and business are bringing people and their cultures together as never before in human history.

The Catholic Church is surely no stranger to this worldwide development. While at times throughout history Catholics have not paid attention to their own preaching by falling into ethnocentrism and racism, overall the church has been, and is today more than ever, a pioneer in intercultural sensibility. The very term "catholic" refers precisely to the church's mission to include all humanity in the loving embrace of a merciful God who desires to reach out to the ends of the earth in a relentless drive to *include* all rather than *exclude* anyone. Two millennia ago, at one of the most critical moments in the fledgling church's history, St. Paul the apostle argued that the Gospel message and membership in the Christian community were open to all, and that to be a follower of Jesus Christ did not require subscribing to Jewish norms and customs nor to those of any other culture. The Christian community was fundamentally open to all as a result of God's *universal love* and the *radical equality of all believers* in and through baptism. Hence the life of the church at all levels—family, parish, and diocese, regionally or universally—has always been characterized by a *negotiation of differences*, giving and receiving, from among the myriad cultures and ways of being, thinking, feeling, and acting as a people. Moreover, this outgoing, inclusive understanding of the church's identity and mission captures the essence of the stunning program of ecclesial reform spearheaded by Pope Francis from the very start of his amazing pontificate. At the heart of it is the Holy Father's invitation to renew the church and the world by building cultures of encounter and dialogue.

After all, openness to culture in all its manifestations and emphasis on dialogue were signature features of the Second Vatican Council, as well as of the refreshing reforms being carried out today by Pope Francis in the spirit of that council fifty years after its closing. Moreover, the recognition of cultural diversity and intercultural effectiveness became priority concerns for the US church that the bishops directly confronted and affirmed when they established in 2008 the Secretariat of Cultural Diversity, for which I served as first executive director. These learnings and reflections flow directly from my experience of the secretariat in its early years.

Within four years of the establishment of the secretariat, two important developments occurred: (1) the Catholic Cultural Diversity Network Convocation took place at the University of Notre Dame in 2010; and (2) coming on the heels of the convocation, a five-module workshop titled *Building Intercultural Competence for Ministers* (BICM) was published and disseminated in 2012. Practical lessons are waiting to be learned by paying attention to the experiences, methods, and contents of these two groundbreaking events. That is why, in the remainder of this chapter, I propose to review the more salient takeaways from the Notre Dame convocation and from the five modules that constitute the BICM workshop because they afford insights into what intercultural competence is all about, map out the territory to be explored, and offer many practical lessons. I will highlight features of these experiences and resources that may be replicated or adapted to the growing number of diverse pastoral and organizational situations found in parishes and dioceses, as well as in Catholic schools, organizations, and apostolic movements. Hopefully, those looking for practical tools, or at least suggestions, will find something of value.

Lessons from the Cultural Diversity Network Convocation

The Notre Dame University gathering brought together a select group of five hundred leaders—lay, religious, and clergy, including several bishops—from six major families of US Catholics: European Americans, Hispanics/Latinos, African Americans, Asian and Pacific Islanders, Native Americans, and migrants, refugees, and travelers. In designing the process, a broad base of participants was invited to give input by means of (a) initial, nationwide consultations with bishops and with existing leadership groups among the six communities identified; and (b) informal surveys of leaders in the field, that is, in shared or multicultural parishes, diocesan offices, schools, seminaries, and Catholic organizations. In assuming leadership in planning the convocation, however, the Secretariat of Cultural Diversity had to overcome a serious obstacle to credibility. Many of the diverse communities perceived the very creation of the secretariat as an instance of a questionable emphasis on "multiculturalism." Let me explain.

The secretariat had come about as the result of merging longstanding secretariats, one for Hispanic affairs and the other for African American affairs. The new secretariat merged those two secretariats and added three other major communities to its purview: Native Americans; Asian and Pacific Islanders; and migrants, refugees, and travelers. A serious and often legitimate criticism of this "multicultural" approach is that it short-circuits the need for the parish, diocese, or organization to establish and maintain *credibility* with the base of these diverse communities. Each cultural group needs its own space to pull itself together in contexts where it has sometimes, or even often, been neglected, overlooked, rendered powerless, or discriminated against. As a result, there is a necessary role for what some call silos—spaces where distinct groups feel comfortable and can process their concerns and build up the necessary experience to engage the wider ecclesial and social reality *from a position of strength* rather than powerlessness. Unity in the church, after all, does not fall down from the sky miraculously. It happens as a result of much prayer and hard work: attitudes, knowledge, and skills that create communion out of the many differences of language, culture, social class, and other forms of diversity character-istic of our times. In creating the Secretariat for Cultural Diversity at the United States Conference of Catholic Bishops (USCCB), the bishops made a prudential judgment that the time was ripe to move to a *second moment* in the realization of communion in diversity. This required bringing cred-ible leaders of the diverse communities into real dialogue (give-and-take) among themselves and with the bishops and their representatives, and maintaining this dynamic among all parties concerned. One of the benefits of moving to this second moment in building up ecclesial communion is the opportunity for all participants to grow in attitudes, knowledge, and skills that support a deepening sense of mutual respect and trust.

A second source of criticism and concern regarding the drive toward "multiculturalism" is that it undercuts the urgent need to identify and raise up credible leaders from the respective ethnic/racial groups. Instead of having its own proper leaders recognized, persons from other groups are often raised up to leadership of these multicultural organizational units. No matter how well-intentioned these leaders may be, they are unable to serve as *role models* to encourage more leadership development in each and every diverse community. Echoing some of the same concerns noted here, the US bishops' Committee on Hispanic Affairs cogently voiced the ongoing concern about a mistaken multicultural way of thinking, as well as of a "one-size-fits-all" mind-set in their 2002 document titled "Encuen-tro and Mission: A Renewed Pastoral Framework for Hispanic Ministry."

Participants in the symposium spoke with concern about a "multicul-tural" model that consolidates minorities under one office, which is headed by a coordinator. In the experience of the participants, this model often di-lutes the identity and vision of Hispanic ministry and those of other ethnic ministries. It can reduce effectiveness in dioceses, parishes, and Catholic organizations and institutions. The leadership in Hispanic ministry is par-ticularly concerned about the reduction of resources and the limited access to the bishop that can follow the establishment of multicultural offices. Also expressed was concern about the exclusion of Hispanic ministry from the decision-making process, particularly in the areas of budgets, plans, and programs specific to Hispanic ministry and its impact on other ministerial areas and in the mission of the church as a whole.[1]

In the same document, Hispanic ministry leaders note that the purpose of multiculturalism is to promote integration and unity among the diverse cultural groups in church and society. As such, multiculturalism is certainly a positive and necessary development. Yet the committee notes:

> Multiculturalism . . . has been critiqued for abetting a "one-size-fits-all" mentality in pastoral ministry by creating a situation in which all groups are put into the same basket. This can have a negative effect on diverse communities by depriving them of the exercise of subsidiarity and of opportunities to form their own leaders and develop appropriate pastoral and educational models, resources and initiatives.[2]

Another criticism of multiculturalism came from the African American community, which noted that emphasis on cultures can eclipse or erode awareness of *racism*, which, despite real gains of the civil rights movement of the 1960s and 1970s, continues to be a reality and matter of serious concern to the church and society. For all these reasons, then, a troublesome level of discomfort and uneasiness among the various ecclesial leaders of the diverse cultural and racial groups had to be reduced, if not eliminated, if the convocation process was to enjoy an adequate level of credibility among all concerned. The path forward, therefore, required those charged with initiating the process, that is, the Secretariat of Cultural Diversity, to demonstrate, as much as possible, an openness to each and every racial/ethnic community, and an ability to listen, learn, and model intercultural effectiveness and mutuality at each step of the way.

Something that contributed mightily to the creation of a sense of mutual regard among the diverse groups was the diverse composition and planning of the Notre Dame convocation's steering committee. Perhaps even more consequential was the composition of the committee on prayer and worship. It was essential that the various groups truly see themselves in the convocation's program of prayer and worship, since this would set the tone for everything else. Much thought was given to this; consequently, among the participants on the committee excellent Hispanic/Latino, African American, Asian and Pacific Islander, Native American, and European American liturgists and musicians were found who knew from real-life experience how to blend elements of the church's sacred liturgy with rituals, symbols, and narratives of the diverse communities, and do so in a respectful, integral, beautiful, and inspiring way.

Perhaps the single most effective method used at the very outset of the encounter was *storytelling*. Each cultural group, including the European

American or Anglo, as it is sometimes called, was asked to reflect on its particular Catholic heritage and express how it lives its Catholicism through rituals, symbols, and narratives unique to it. Something very interesting occurred when the groups went to discuss their particular ways of being Catholic, of bringing faith and church teaching to life. The various non-European groups, including the African Americans, went at it with gusto and found great joy and pride in reviewing their customs and distinctive styles of Catholicism.

If truth be told, however, the European American group was a bit stumped. The task seemed somewhat awkward or strange to them for a couple of reasons. First, because the European Americans were simply used to thinking of their way of being Catholic as virtually the only way: they were the "insiders," as it were, and the other cultural groups were the "outsiders." This in itself was a revelation for the European American group, which discovered that the convocation process did not simply assume that the traditional US way of doing things was *the* norm, much less the only way to proceed, but simply *a* norm in a church that de facto is a communion of diversity. The European Americans discovered what it's like to *level the field* by becoming simply one group among many. The experience of being an outsider can be a revelation. Perhaps another reason for some European American participants feeling "stretched" by the experience was that US Catholicism is very driven by the enforcement of standards. It is a very post-Tridentine Catholicism that may suffer from rigidity and from too much organization, standardization, and concern with rules. Many other forms of Catholicism lived by persons of other cultures are more spontaneous and *expressive*. They bring a rich aesthetic orientation, imagination, color, movement, affectivity, and sense of celebration to their Catholicism. Tendencies toward rigidity and inflexibility—what Bishop Robert Barron calls "beigeness"—hold some forms of Catholicism back from achieving a truly *inculturated evangelization*, which goes well beyond simply engaging the mind or keeping the rules.

Thus the promotion of intercultural competencies has everything to do with bringing the faith to life, giving real traction to what we believe by expressing it in captivating stories, gestures, rituals, and symbols instead of reducing it to the banality of standard norms and practices in the name of order or orthodoxy—what Pope Francis calls "turning the church into a tidy museum."

A practical question that arose during the convocation had to do with the need for every parish, diocese, school, and organization to ask how willing it was to treat "outside" cultures with respect and even mutuality. Without doing so, one does not get to first base in intercultural relations. It has been observed that sometimes a genuine sense of hospitality in Catholic parishes is only skin deep. People say "welcome," but they place a serious condition on it: namely, that the newcomers fit in and conform to the host community's way of doing things, to their social class sensibilities or other distinctions. True interculturality and hospitality—in a Christian sense, at least—requires real openness to the *other* based on love and an ability to both *give* to others and *receive* from what they have to offer. It is not merely a matter of tolerance or "going along in order to get along." This realization marked the interaction among all the cultural groups to a notable degree at the convocation.

Mapping the Road to Intercultural Competence: What to Do

The first part of this chapter has tried to convey the idea that growth in intercultural competence requires careful thought and planning, but most especially a *change of attitude.* Responding to diversity in one's parish or in the diocese is not just a matter of "being nice" to others or engaging in a kind of hospitality that is skin deep. This second part outlines specific strategies and activities that are deeply *challenging* because they promote growth in cognitive, affective, and behavioral skills and characteristics that support effective and appropriate interaction in various cultural contexts. Yes, they require change in mind-sets and approaches to ministry in the concrete situations in which ministry is carried out. Some of these recommendations are general, others more specific, but all of them require imagination and an ability to take risks, or what Pope Francis likes to call "going out," leaving the security of the sacristy for the dangers of the street and risking "getting into an accident."

One place to begin is by simply formulating, reflecting on, and sharing answers about key questions that affect the depth and quality of the individual or collective response to the challenges of intercultural encounters. These questions provide an opportunity to highlight at least some of the contents and practical methods found in the above-mentioned USCCB BICM workshop. First, I will look at the all-important question of attitude—what has been called *heart-set.* Second, I will outline what kind of knowledge or *mind-set* must be acquired and enhanced. And third, I will profile some practical skills or *skill-sets* required for intercultural effectiveness. These three categories provide the *analytic tools* for properly assessing what to do, where to start, and where one wants to go in the development of intercultural sensibility.

Developing the Right Attitudes

1. *Curiosity*: The literature on intercultural competence insists that one of the more important attitudes necessary to engage others, *any* others, is curiosity. Strange as it may sound, efforts to develop intercultural capacities rise and fall on this principle. Without a true desire to *experience and know the reality of the other*, efforts to reach out in any form are "dead in the water." The sad truth is that some people simply lack curiosity, and hence they remain locked in self-referentiality and, let me use the proper word, *ignorance*. (My father used to say, "Ignorance is bliss!") In a world of rising diversity, there are many who cannot bear the cost of reaching out for various reasons. A heart-set of curiosity must be cultivated if the parish, diocese, or wider church is ever to become a real force for evangelization.

2. *Bias, prejudice, stereotypes, and racism*: Here are four complicated attitudes or ways of feeling and thinking that create often insurmountable obstacles and effectively cut off people from one another. These frequently deadly orientations are often, if not usually, held by people in an unconscious and unanalyzed way. Strange as it may sound, the more religious people are, the more embedded these negativities can be. Module 4 of BICM develops this theme and provides simple group activities that will help ministers identify and moderate these deeply rooted but toxic tendencies in all human beings. These attitudes are perpetual "elephants in our ecclesial living rooms." One of the first attitudes that must be overcome is the one that suggests that because we are a church community of faithful, good Christians, such negative tendencies could not possibly be found within us. Yet the recognition of these negative tendencies is so important for the Christian community at all times and places because it puts flesh and bones onto our assertion about the reality of our own personal sinfulness and how sin functions structurally, as well in the church as an institution, and also in civil society.

3. *Living with ambiguity*: It goes without saying that exposure to the reality of cultural differences means confronting the fact that human beings deal with all kinds of important life situations in a variety of ways that may even seem strange and puzzling. People usually want clear and straightforward answers and are uncomfortable with whatever is different or *other*.

Differences of language, race, culture, political ideology, and social class often elicit fear. Cultural competence requires an ability to live with these fears and strangenesses—it comes with the territory—in a global church and world. Unity in the parish or church is not the result of denying or rejecting these differences, but of working through them to achieve communion in *diversity* rather than communion in *conformity*.

Developing Our Knowledge

1. *Culture*: Understanding what is meant by "culture" is the single most important key for grasping the church's contemporary understanding of its identity and mission today. Too many good Catholics, including some church leaders, seemed to be challenged by the anthropological conception of culture as "the way of thinking, feeling, and acting shared by a people." Understanding religion depends on understanding culture, because culture is the way we human beings are who and what we are. At the heart of this idea of culture are stories, rituals, and symbols that are the powerful *building blocks of meaning* in people's lives. Module 2 of BICM provides a handy overview of this foundational bit of knowledge for appreciating why insight into cultures and how they work is so essential to *inculturated evangelization*—the church's mission.

In addition to the broad concept of culture, however, intercultural sensibilities require a deeper knowledge of how diverse cultures think about themselves and the world around them. For instance, do they take a *collectivist* or an *individualist* approach to human experience? Are they more feminine or masculine in how they approach experience and decision-making? Do they prize hierarchy or "pecking orders," or do they prefer co-responsible arrangements that level differences among generations, genders, rich and poor, and so forth? Another defining characteristic of cultures is whether they exhibit and honor the customs and norms of the community's past, of its ancestors. Or are they modern or postmodern, future-oriented and unaware or unconcerned about preserving values from the past? How do diverse cultures relate to time? Is punctuality valued, or are relationships so important that they trump punctuality?

2. *Immersion and language experiences*: Finally, a knowledge of other cultures, languages, and religions learned by formal study or personal encounters is important. Personal experience—often as the result of taking risks—is the most important way to grow in intercultural sensibility. *Im-*

mersion experiences, for example, can be gained by travel within or outside the United States, but also by careful attention to the places where diverse cultures thrive right next door to us in virtually all US metropolitan and suburban centers. Neither the territoriality of the parish or diocese nor the limited audience of Catholic schools, organizations, and movements exonerates any of those particular units of the church from the mission to reach out and be as inclusive as possible.

Developing Skills

1. *Communication skills*: Effective communication demands that one truly know the one being addressed. One must know, for instance, whether the person or group being addressed belongs to an individualist or a collectivist culture. Even more pertinent is what happens when an individualist culture, like that of the United States, encounters collectivist cultures like those of Asia, Africa, and Latin America. The individualist culture sees life as a process of advancement for the individual person, while collectivist cultures see life as a matter of advancing the well-being of the family and community, not the individual. The BICM workshop provides a more comprehensive overview, which I suggest reading. Simply put, ignorance of these differences can lead to huge mistakes by pastors and lay ministers, along with failures to effectively communicate, persuade, and lead.

2. *Face management*: Flowing from the differences between collectivist and individualist cultures is the matter of "face." Saving face is a major concern in many Asian as well as other traditional African and Latin American cultures. This involves attitudes toward elders and ancestors as well as toward hierarchy and authority. Matters of gender relations may also be part of this. Intercultural sensibility demands a basic level of exposure to and insight about how all these complex cultural sensibilities function and interact in today's world.

3. *Conducting meetings and reaching decisions*: Involved here are conflicting attitudes toward the purpose of meetings. Traditional cultures do not think of them primarily as "getting something done." Rather, meetings are mainly about the cultivation of human relationships *for their own sake*. This is the contrast between cultures that stress *doing* (our modern and postmodern developed world) and others that focus on *being*. This is not a matter of right or wrong; it is simply about differences. In decision-making, modern cultures tend toward a *democratic*, "take a vote and the majority

wins" approach, while many collectivist, traditional cultures prefer a *consensus* approach that seeks to leave out no one.

4. *Leadership and conflict resolution*: In modern, individualist cultures, leaders are chosen because they can "get things done." In some collectivist cultures they are chosen because of the *relationship* they have by reason of age or family heritage, rank, or status. Approaches to conflict vary from individualist to collectivist cultures. Individualist cultures see conflicts in terms of issues and seek to address differences directly. Collectivist cultures look first to relationships, not issues, because the most desired outcome is not resolving some issue or other, but maintaining good "group face." Hence, being direct in one's communication can be inappropriate and ineffective.

Conclusion

Navigating the complex reality of cultures is not only, or mainly, a matter of skills, but of attitude and spirituality. One needs to be *converted* to the reality of the other; one needs to truly be motivated. Pope Francis is doing his part with his revolution, shaking things up with his calls for an *inclusive* rather than an exclusive church, one that always reaches out to others. But such outreach has consequences. Among them is the need to do our homework and get to work. These pages have focused on analytical tools and a few practical suggestions on how to go about doing that work.

The culture of encounter and dialogue proposed by Pope Francis is as old as the Gospel itself. Our Argentine pope did not invent the idea of the absolute centrality of encounter and dialogue for the well-being of the church. These realities have everything to do with the trinitarian, incarnate God we have come to know in Jesus of Nazareth. At this moment in human history, the Catholic Church, precisely because it is "catholic," is being invited and challenged as never before by this pope—"from the ends of the earth"—to pay witness to God's universal love by modeling intercultural sensibility and competence. The conditions are more than ripe for doing this. The Catholic Church in the United States has a privileged role in responding to this challenge, given its history as a refuge for immigrants that is one of the deepest and most authentic currents of both our Catholic and American identities.

Endnotes

1. "Encuentro and Mission: A Renewed Pastoral Framework for Hispanic Ministry," in *A New Beginning: Hispanic/Latino Ministry—Past, Present, Future* (Washington, DC: USCCB, 2012), 69.

2. *Building Intercultural Competence for Ministers* (Washington, DC: USCCB, 2012), 42. Another excellent resource is *Best Practices for Shared Parishes: So That They May All Be One* (Washington, DC: USCCB, 2013).

5
Intergenerational Ministry

Nicole Perone

Many a well-meaning parishioner has wrung their hands as they ask, "Where are all the young people?" Of course, as a seminarian (and for many, a young adult at the same time), you have probably had this well-intentioned query directed your way. Your pastoral ministry will be abundant with encounters with young people, internal to the parish experience and beyond the boundary of the church walls. Whether or not your ministerial assignment formally involves the community's youth or young adult ministries, to care for and engage the young people in our midst is the sacred responsibility of all members of the body of Christ. Certainly, there are ample statistics on disaffiliation and data on young adult engagement available; however, ministering to young people requires a sense of imagination that sees beyond what might be dismaying data into a new hope.

I would like to provide some guideposts for you as you look toward a pastoral future of ministries to and with young people. While these are not exhaustive, I hope they will provide some sense of pastoral best practices. Instead of considering them through the lens of what should *not* be done (for these are not commandments!), I would like to propose some ways our ministries with young people can be blessed.

Blessed Are They Who Recall That Christ Alone Is the Savior

One of the sagest pieces of ministerial wisdom that I was ever given was: *"Remember that there are two fundamental truths: (1) there is a God;*

(2) you are not him!" It evokes a chuckle, but there is a great need for this adage. It is easy for us, in ministry, to fall victim to a complex singularly focused on winning souls as though we are the exclusive wagers of spiritual battle. However, it is Christ that wins souls, not us. Seminary or ministerial formation does not equate to being "smarter" in the faith than anyone—our faith is not a subject to ace, but a journey to walk together.

Additionally, when we allow Christ to be the Savior and not us, we are truly set free from that divine burden—free to fulfill our vocations and let the Holy Spirit work. As a priest, you are not meant to be solely in the role of teacher or bearer of sacraments at all hours—your role is also to be the shepherd. Perhaps you might have some experience with this distinct farm job in your family, or have witnessed shepherds on a pilgrimage to the Holy Land: what is key for this conversation is that, while occasionally a shepherd must defend the flock or tend to a sick lamb, the majority of a shepherd's work is to simply be among his flock. That presence is everything to sheep who look to their shepherd.

Finally, it is a simple truth that our ministries are better when we work together. A commitment to co-responsibility models a new way of being co-workers in the vineyard of the Lord.

Blessed Are They Who Celebrate the Adventure of Being Young, from Within and Without

What to Know about Young People

I will avoid going too deeply into particular generational qualities of young people today, because it will most certainly age this section poorly! However, there are some truths we can hold up to the light about young people today, and young people throughout time, that will inform how we can celebrate this *"original and stimulating stage of life, which Jesus himself experienced, thereby sanctifying it"* (*Christus Vivit* 22).[1]

"Young people" is a phrase which is inclusive of both youth and young adults. First, it is worth noting the age differences as defined by the church in the United States: when referring to youth, we mean those under the age of 18. When referring to young adults, we mean those from age 18 to 39. Of course, the latter has some fluidity: when does adulthood truly begin (beyond the legal definition)? When does "young" adulthood truly end? These are broader questions that are worth exploring, and have been done elsewhere, so I will not belabor them—but they will resurface as we explore serving young people.

Young adulthood has specific needs to which we, as church, should be attentive. It is an extremely transitional period. In that window of 18 to 39 years of age, young adults will enter and graduate from college; begin their first job—and likely change jobs multiple times; move out of their family home; perhaps move to a new city—or more than one; start building communities of friends; discern their call to marriage, priesthood, or religious life; if the former, start dating and perhaps find their partner; have children and grow their families; experience the aging and losses of loved ones; and so much more. That is a tremendous amount of life to live in that span of time!

The generations which are currently young are the most formally educated and the most informed—it is no surprise, as digital natives, that they have the most access to information, and quickly. They are also significantly driven by matters of justice, with a keen sense of right and wrong. Contrary to popular opinion, they are also quite spiritual, and their possession of a spirituality (even if it is undefined in our traditional religious sense) is something into which we can dial and build a connection. They are very much in discernment of their vocations, but may not use that vocabulary. They are exploring the questions of: Why am I here? What are my gifts? What am I meant to do? How am I going to contribute to the world? (Of course, the church is rich in tools to respond to those needs! More on that later.) Furthermore, the two highest-value qualities to young people are *authenticity* and *vulnerability*, which breed credibility. Emulating these qualities will look a bit different for each person and each context.

Your Youthfulness Is a Gift!

As you are reading this, you might be experiencing a bit of cognitive dissonance; the majority of seminarians in the United States are, themselves, young adults. To be in the demographic to which you are ministering can be tricky to navigate, but not impossible. In this context, this is profoundly experiential—your experience of being young can draw you in to a particular understanding of the young people you serve. Young people are naturally drawn to other young people—they may have in common the same desires and struggles, and experiences of transitions. For you, it is a gift to be with people your age and (somewhat!) your stage of life, who care about the church, who are passionate and thoughtful and navigating the waters of faith and life.

As all things in life require, a tension is needed here: while you may, in fact, be a young adult currently, you and your friends/peers are not necessarily representative or typical of all young people. Reflect for a moment on your family of origin, your upbringing in the faith (or not), and your own journey to get to this point. As multifaceted as your own story is, so goes the faith journey of every single young person you will serve. *You can honor your own identity as a young adult (or a recent young adult) without giving it primacy of place as a model—it is A truth, not THE truth.* Making space for the young adult journey of others while grappling with your own is not only possible, but profound! That tension is formation at work, and it something to which we are all called throughout life.

Healthy Ministerial Boundaries as a Tool of Profound Relationships

Just because some factors between you and your young peers are different (which we will address shortly) does not mean all friendly relationships are forbidden. Relationships with your fellow young adults concurrent with your priestly ministry can be very life-giving if you allow yourself to love others as they are. It can be easier and seemingly safer to give in to fear—but do not fear them, just love them!

Of course, this is not to discount the crucial nature of healthy ministerial boundaries, especially between a young adult priest and his young adult peers in the community. This is not a mandate not to be relational or build genuine friendships; however, hold carefully the truth that ministry presents a power difference. Thus, *you cannot truly be peers if you are in a ministerial role in others' lives, but you can be in relationship.* "Healthy" ministerial boundaries do not mean "all or nothing"—it means healthy! You, as a seminarian, can contribute to laying the building blocks of healthy ministerial boundaries by cultivating confidence in your vocation, engaging in platonic intimate human friendships, and strengthening your social awareness of where lines are that ought not to be crossed. These may look different in varied situations, but one consistent factor is that the parish can be the nucleus of those holistic, appropriate, life-giving experiences of relationship.

In the end, it is fully possible to celebrate the adventure of being young together with the young people in your community of faith.

Blessed Are They Who Celebrate the Contributions of All the Faithful with an Intergenerational and Intercultural Spirit

Avoiding Tokenization

It is tempting, when ministering with young adults, to want to plug them in to every single aspect of parish life with great enthusiasm. Of course, young people can and absolutely should be part of leading in every aspect of parish life! However, it is important to *maintain a discerning spirit and ask the Lord exactly where a young person's gifts might be best suited to benefit the Christian community.* Insisting on having a young adult on every committee or in every parish ministry is a nice idea but ignores whether or not the young people in question feel called to serve in that way. It sells short their gifts and potential for meaningful contribution, because to have the "token young adult" delegitimizes what they are bringing to the table.

Tokenization can also swing in the opposite direction, and take the form of age-specific ministries. Although there has been some sense of success around gatherings such as Theology on Tap or Holy Hour for young adults, these are not the exclusive avenues of engagement for young people. Although young people are in a communal stage of life and desire an experience of community, it can take many forms—whether young-couple dinners, group experiences of service, plugging into the parish Bible study or adult faith-formation offerings, and yes, even Theology on Tap!

Tokenization can also take the form of overdoing it in the "cultural immersion" of youth. While it can be very helpful to understand cultural references and their role in the lives of young people (one campus minister never scheduled events for the same night as when *Game of Thrones* was on in the 2010s, because they knew they would lose attendees!), to overdo it is to drown out any chance of meaningful connection in the sea of attempted relevancy. "Twitter priests" fall victim to the same fate. Being present on social media just for the sake of being there is not a "good enough" reason—digital discernment is paramount for digital discipleship, but that is another topic for another time. Basically, *don't overdo something for the sake of being "hip" or "cool" with the young people in your community*—it is not sustainable.

Celebrating the Gifts

It is a truth we can hold dear that contribution in the Christian community is not exclusively proportionate to age. Wisdom is not exclusive to those who are more seasoned in age; young people have a myriad of gifts, both spiritual and temporal, to contribute to the church and the world. Of course, a community cannot succeed when it relies singularly on one generation or another for filling the pews, staffing the ministries, or attending events. To minister intergenerationally is to remember and celebrate that wisdom which Pope Francis shared in *Christus Vivit*:

> During the Synod, one of the young auditors from the Samoan Islands spoke of the Church as a canoe, in which the elderly help to keep on course by judging the position of the stars, while the young keep rowing, imagining what waits for them ahead. Let us steer clear of young people who think that adults represent a meaningless past, and those adults who always think they know how young people should act. Instead, let us all climb aboard the same canoe and together seek a better world, with the constantly renewed momentum of the Holy Spirit. (201)

As a priest, your welcome by the older members of the parish will be robust and joyful—regrettably, your young peers are not always afforded that welcome. Countless young adults have experienced a closed door, a stern frown, a snide comment, or a barrier to entry. Instead, we have the chance to be the church we want to see! Encouraging those who are already "in" the community to be gracious, hospitable, and kind to those who are "without" will provide for the gateway moments that young people experience to be more welcoming and Spirit-filled.

Lines are not only drawn in communities by age, but also by culture. The communities you serve in your priestly ministry will encompass a variety of cultures, languages, and experiences. Special attention should be paid to the reality that Hispanics/Latinos comprise 40 percent of Catholics in the US, and Hispanic/Latino young people are the fastest growing population in the church. Appreciating the significant presence and substantive contribution of those communities will ensure a more vibrant community of faith that benefits from their gifts, especially in terms of young people.

Blessed Are They Who Cultivate Spirits of Discernment

As previously mentioned, we know that young people occupy a state of life that is rife with experiences of discernment. At each stage and transitional moment, they are asking the big questions: *Why am I here? What are my gifts? What am I meant to do? How am I going to contribute to the world?* From our faith-based perspective, we know that these questions point to an understanding of our own vocations—who God created us to be and how God desires us to use those gifts. What a sacred opportunity we have to journey with young people in their discernment and equip them with the tools to undertake it well! To name what young people are going through, share where we see the workings of the Holy Spirit, and offer ways their experiences contribute to their journey can be some of the most formative contributions we can make.

This requires us to *emulate what we advocate*. As a priest, you have a responsibility in your own spiritual life to be attentive to the discernment of spirits, to model best spiritual practices, and let the fruit borne from that process testify to its value in the lives of young people. This also requires us to let go of the incomplete correlation of the word "vocation" with "priest/religious recruitment"—a hard habit to break! Of course, we know that the state of life to which we are called—the priesthood, religious or consecrated life, marriage, the single life, etc.—is a very important component of our vocation, but not the entirety. Just so, young people are in the very weeds of learning that truth: that there are many pieces to the mosaic that composes the person God created them to be. What a privilege to walk with them as they discover those pieces.

Blessed Are They Who Lead with a Pastoral Heart

Accompaniment

To truly minister to and with young people, you must start from a place of accompaniment. You might be thinking that this has become quite a buzzword in the church lately, but it holds especially true for young people. By not objectifying young people as a commodity or prize to be won but honoring their unique needs (without forcing them into a certain mold) and being willing to journey with them as they figure this life out, we can help them make great strides for the kingdom of God and their relationship with Jesus Christ.

To be walked with—not led like an animal on leash, but walked alongside as a friend in Christ—can be a profoundly special experience. Take just a moment to think of those who have walked alongside you on your journey, and how their presence in your life impacted it. *True accompaniment is modeled after the resurrected Christ who met his disciples on the road to*

Emmaus; he acknowledged their sorrow, listened to their stories, and walked with them on the road—even in the wrong direction. This can be challenging for us, for sure, but it will bear much greater fruit than attempting to drag them in the "right" direction. Starting from where young people are and going from there has a much higher chance of success than setting an unreachable bar and commanding, "Jump!"

Forming Relationships

As you have probably learned well and experienced personally, pastoral ministry is incomplete without the building of relationships. Young people are especially relational, and in a period of life that is profoundly communal in nature. Therefore, *as a priest, you will have a sacred opportunity to build meaningful, live-giving relationships with young people that will offer them a prophetic, compassionate witness of the God who loves them.*

Allow me to underscore one of those adjectives: choosing compassion over pity for young people heals the distance they may feel from the church. A critical mandate of the Holy Father is for us to go out to the margins, to seek those who are not already in our flock to share the love of Christ with them. As it pertains to young people, this includes those who seem to disagree with us, or who disaffiliate from the church. In forming relationships with those particular young people, we remove the barrier of the "other" and present a new way: relationship between beloved children of God.

To be clear, this building of relationships must be stripped of preconceived notions and a "right versus wrong" mentality. When we posture like we have all of the answers, it turns off young people and inhibits ability to build relationship—young people smell inauthenticity a mile away! Instead of insisting on a posture of teaching and conferring your wisdom on the unknowing, I would propose instead offering an experience of the living God. Modeling the lived experience of this truth is vastly more compelling than any word that can be preached or written. Relationship with you can, and will, lead to deepening relationship with Christ and the church.

Relationships cultivate a sense of inclusivity. You cannot exclude those with whom you are in relationship. Inclusivity truly matters to young people so they have an authentic experience of being invited, valued, and wanted at the table. To infuse that sense of inclusion ensures the investment of young people in the Christian community.

Blessed Are They Who Avoid Absolutes and Polarization

When ministering to young people, it serves us all well to remember that young people come in all shapes, sizes, perspectives, and places on the journey—let's just say that there are more than Baskin-Robbins' thirty-one flavors! By assuming they "definitely" like this or "must" believe that, we draw hard lines that cannot be crossed and certainly aren't compelling to come near. It is a safe pastoral practice to live in the in-between and avoid absolutes, for the very simple reason that *you never know the whole story of someone in front of you*. A hard line that you take could, unintentionally, make someone feel unwelcome or drive them away, when your desire is for them to draw closer to Christ through deeper relationship with his church.

Of course, absolutes go hand-in-hand with polarization: the most effective tool of the evil one to divide the church. Simply put, *polarization is not and cannot be the work of the Holy Spirit!* Whether on social media or in Catholic media spheres (where camps are firmly planted as polar opposites), young people are watching how we treat one another and asking themselves: "If this is how they treat their own 'in-crowd' Catholics, how will they treat me?" It is no wonder that young people turn away in horror when they witness our own toxic discourse!

One way to combat polarization is to start within our own hearts. It is natural that each of us has our perspectives and opinions and operates from those places. It makes us human. However, as the shepherd of a flock, your call will be to "smell like your sheep"—in this case, to ensure that you represent well the people you serve. When you become part of a community, you need to understand from whence all the people come, and meet them where they are. They will be your spiritual family. When you are given an assignment, learn as much as possible about the local ministerial context in which you will serve, and do not bring your baggage or preconceived notions there. Get to know their local "flavor" of Catholicism—this might mean that your consumption of Catholic media needs to adapt to that context, too.

Blessed Are They Who Know That Hard Questions Cannot Be Solved with Simple Answers

In ministry, but especially with young people, "because the church says so" and other simplistic answers are the fastest way to lose credibility. Young people do seek answers, but also seek the freedom to grapple with difficult questions and realities. This is precisely the freedom that God created us to enjoy! God did not desire for us to be mindless robots, mechanically programmed to do his will without thought. God wants us to know, love, and serve God with our whole beings, letting our lives be a resounding YES! Cultivating a healthy spirituality and conscience in young people will give church guidance fertile ground to take root and bear fruit. A priest who walks with young people must *acknowledge the gray areas and a changing world*, as well as changing life stages and situations, knowing that he cannot control their decision-making but can offer a way to the fullness of life in Christ.

Of course, this is not to say that there are not some kinds of answers our faith can offer in response to hard questions. Young people do crave answers—but more in response to navigating the transitions and traumas of life. When they behold suffering, they are going to ask why, and here is the difficult truth: you, their priest, do not have the answers. You can invite them to know Christ's peace—to know that *his humanity is our consolation and his divinity is our hope*—but at the end of the day, the answers are not on you to provide. (See the earlier point about the Savior!)

Resources for Ministering with Young People

Christus Vivit: Post-Synodal Apostolic Exhortation of the Holy Father Francis to Young People and to the Entire People of God. Pope Francis, 2019.

Final Report: National Dialogue on Catholic Pastoral Ministry with Youth and Young Adults. National Federation for Catholic Youth Ministry, 2021

Sons and Daughters of the Light: A Pastoral Plan for Ministry with Young Adults. USCCB, 1996. https://www.usccb.org/beliefs-and-teachings/who-we-teach/young-adults/sons-and-daughters-of-light.

Organizations:

Catholic Campus Ministry Association
LaRED—National Catholic Network de Pastoral Juvenil Hispana
National Institute for Ministry with Young Adults
National Federation for Catholic Youth Ministry
USCCB—Youth and Young Adult Ministries
V Encuentro

Endnote

1. Pope Francis, *Christus Vivit*, To Young People and to the Entire People of God (March 25, 2019), emphasis added.

6

Recruiting and Managing Volunteers

Nicole Perone

It is no secret that volunteers are, in many settings, the animating force of parish life. In a time when there are few full-time parish employees (and declining numbers of priests and religious to supplement staffing), faith communities everywhere rely on those members of the faithful who are willing to volunteer their time, energy, and gifts in service to the community they love. They are the ones that are on the front lines of evangelization, catechesis, and social action, going out on mission in the spirit of the apostles. What a blessing that is for us!

This particular model can be of invaluable support to a pastoral team, but it is not without its challenges. Certainly, overseeing parish volunteers means managing time, expectations, and personalities, as well as needing to understand more deeply the value of volunteer ministry. As priests, you can expect lay volunteers to be the most significant proportion of your collaborators for the entirety of your priestly ministry. (Even when there is significant paid parish staffing, volunteers are abundant.) Knowing that volunteers will compose the primary team with which you will work and serve, it is helpful to think about how to manage volunteers effectively.

When inviting, managing, or collaborating with volunteers, it is always a worthwhile starting point to consider the mission of the ministry in question. Each volunteer ministry is, in fact, a ministry—even if not in a formal fashion instituted by the church, or paid as a professional track— and therefore has a particular mission. Just so, every parish has a distinct sense of mission, perhaps a charism, that sets it apart. While we know that the parish is the conduit for the mission of the church to be lived, each community does so in its own distinct way. Articulating the mission of your parish and what makes it special is the first step to understanding the mission of the volunteer ministries therein.

Once you have determined the particular ethos of your parish, then I invite you to consider the volunteer ministries. Understanding the mission of each will set you up for success in manifesting that mission through the volunteers. I invite you to consider a volunteer ministry—perhaps one you were involved in in your childhood parish, or one you engaged with during a pastoral year. What would you say was its mission? That question may seem simple, but I invite you to peel one layer off and go deeper.

You might have thought of the parish fair. Perhaps your mind conjured up that the purpose of the many volunteer ministries at the fair is to execute the annual event, or bring in some revenue for the parish. Those may well be the first purposes that come to mind, and they aren't inherently bad, but dive deeper. Is the mission of the parish fair *exclusively* to bring in some extra revenue, or is it to offer a family-friendly outing in the midst of the summer for the community when not much else is available? Is it to bring the people of the community together for food and fun, something lighthearted that brings people from around town to the parish grounds? Is it to offer something for the community that is not available in other places? Thinking just one layer deeper than the obvious purpose can help bore down to the heart of the mission of the ministry.

You might have thought of the parish religious education ministry. The purpose would be to catechize the children of the parish—certainly a vital mission! But let's give that some depth: the mission of being a volunteer catechist at the parish is to introduce young people to Jesus Christ, to show them the value of a relationship with him, to accompany adolescents as they learn and grow in their faith. Drilling down a layer or two can be helpful for this process and gives these volunteer ministries some gravitas.

Another way to explore a volunteer ministry's mission is to ask the question: How does this ministry bring Jesus Christ to people? Maybe it's through building up the Christian community through social events; perhaps it's through acts of justice and charity, living Matthew 25. This exercise is helpful for you as the priest who accompanies these volunteers: it will equip you with the understanding and tools to recruit, engage, form, and retain volunteers.

I would invite you to consider volunteer recruitment less as a method of accruing "warm bodies" to fill a need, but more as an invitation to others to be part of the mission in a way that engages the gifts God gave them.

This does require developing a spirit of discernment in the parish (another conversation for another time), but doing so helps the people of the community understand the gifts that God has given them, where their strengths are, and how those gifts can be used to glorify God and bring about the Christian community.

For example, it would be imprudent to ask someone in the parish whose skill set does not include numbers or math to staff the cash register at the parish fair, or to ask someone who is quite introverted and shy to be an usher or greeter! It is not a referendum on anyone, but simply not a good use of their gifts when there are other options. It is a matter of being honest about how each person was created by God and where their skills lie. That sort of intentionality will lead to greater recruiting and retention of volunteers.

Another truth of parish volunteer ministry is the invaluable nature of the personal ask. When an announcement is made from the pulpit to the general congregation, or a generic ask is printed in the bulletin, most people will not self-select. However, when someone is personally approached and their qualities are identified to them as having been noticed and appreciated, that intentionality is disarming and engaging in equal measure.

From the first invitation to a decade of service, managing expectations for volunteers is a critical component of the process—and it begins with you. First, I encourage you to be honest with yourself about the capacities of a volunteer. Recall that, by definition, they are not paid to do this job! Tailor your expectations to be commensurate with the volunteer ministry itself, and begin from a place of gratitude that they are even willing to be a part of the ministry altogether. It can be challenging to be grateful in the face of limitations that volunteers present, but an attitude of gratitude is always the appropriate starting point.

Moving outward to volunteers, here are a few simple tips for managing their expectations:

- *Be candid.* Be honest about what is expected. It is reasonable to be positive and want to draw volunteers into how wonderful and valuable the ministry is, but do not sugarcoat it in the hopes of getting a "yes." If it requires physical labor or driving, say so; if it takes place on evenings or weekends, say so. Even more specifically, don't sell short the amount of time and energy a volunteer ministry requires. It's unfair to people who have demands on their lives outside of the parish, and it is unfair to the ministry itself because that leads to much greater attrition.

- *Be clear.* Being clear about as much as possible in advance—such as the number of hours or days a volunteer ministry will take, the amount of driving, autonomy versus oversight by parish staff, how many other people will share the load of responsibility, and if anything is expected to change (e.g., ramping up hours of work in the days closest to a major event)—will be much appreciated. If someone is even entering into the conversation with you about volunteering in an amenable fashion, they will be more grateful and more likely to hear you out if you are clear.

- *Be continuously communicative.* Keep sharing those expectations, and if they should change throughout the timeline of engagement. Ideally, the expectations stated clearly should not change too much throughout, but we know life is not that easy, and communicating changes—and, if possible, why the changes occurred—can be helpful for managing the expectations of volunteers. This way, there are no surprises!

When people say "yes" to a volunteer ministry in a parish, they are doing so out of some degree of love: for the parish, for the ministry that has meant something to them, for the people they serve with, or even for you, their priest. The gift you can give in response to that love is managing the expectations in honest, clear, and communicative fashion.

If there is clarity in what is expected, engagement will be fairly consistent because of that strong foundation. Of course, life is going to continue to happen within the parish and external to it, and so engagement will have a natural course of flow. Certainly, we would love every volunteer to be as enthusiastic about a ministry as we are!

Managing engagement requires consistent pastoral accompaniment of volunteers. They are not extensions of your ministerial responsibilities that do not need attention; regardless of the ministries entrusted to them, they will still be members of your flock and you their shepherd, even if you are both hauling boxes of canned goods for the soup kitchen or stuffing envelopes for the fundraising campaign. Do not allow the need to complete tasks or move ministries along obscure that in your sight. What is going on in their lives? What barriers to deeper engagement might need your assistance to be removed?

Of course, others are going to come into volunteer ministries swinging, and their engagement will be off the charts—and it might not be the passion project of everyone else! Some might want to engage with greater intensity than you, or the parish, can match—which can be difficult, because you do not want to stifle enthusiasm, but it speaks to our previous point of candor in expectation.

Management of people in any setting requires an attentiveness to the myriad personalities before you. There will be every personality type who comes forward to volunteer in your parish; some will be easier to gel with than others. Unfortunately, it could fall to you, in your pastoral role, to manage those personalities. We can charitably assume that everyone involved in parish ministry means well, but for a variety of reasons—some of which might be age, cultural differences, or just a spectrum of social acumen—some volunteers may not always get along with everyone.

Whether it's an overexuberant volunteer who wants to get things done yesterday and bangs down the pastor's door, or a needy volunteer who wants to gripe on the phone constantly, or a passive volunteer who needs consistent direction and doesn't naturally take initiative, there will be many types who will test the patience of their fellow volunteers as well as their clergy. There will not be just one way to manage your volunteers' personalities. As James Joyce said, the Catholic Church means "here comes everybody," and that is precisely what you will get in a faith community—everybody. To navigate this will require an intentionality on your part as the shepherd: knowing the personalities at play and plugging them in where appropriate, how to accompany them to navigate certain circumstances and mediate conflict where you can.

No matter how absurd the dramatics or hilarious the hijinks might be, I encourage you to operate with charity towards all volunteers. In recent years, there has become a culture of mocking "parish ladies" or "Susan from the parish council" in ministerial corners of the internet and social media. While it is certainly helpful to blow off steam when frustrated, or workshop some ways to solve conflict with trusted friends, a mentor, or a support group, I exhort you not to allow the craziness of human conflict to permeate your role as the priest in the community. Tempting though it can be, you will have a distinct responsibility to rise above the fray and stand *in persona Christi* not just sacramentally, but in community as well.

In the immortal words of the book of Ecclesiastes, "For everything there is a season." Some people are aware of the way those seasons in their lives ebb and flow, and others are less aware or less receptive. Perhaps a volunteer is moving out of town, away from the parish; perhaps they are retiring from their full-time job, or becoming a caretaker for children or aging parents; or, sometimes, something external is not inducing the end of a season of volunteering, but something internal is. Whatever the impetus, it happens to all of us.

We fall victim to the quandary of moving on very easily in parish life: in many situations, volunteers will be involved in a ministry for a really long time—perhaps even decades! (That can be a gift, because institutional memory is really important and long-term investment can be wonderful. Sometimes it can be a challenge, because a vice grip over time suffocates.) Many of us have probably heard some iteration of this line from a well-meaning volunteer: "I've been doing the [insert ministry here] for thirty-five years!" and it doesn't raise their eyebrows in the way it does yours.

The moment will inevitably arrive when someone wants, needs, or is forced by circumstances beyond their control to move on from a volunteer ministry. Better that we are prepared to navigate it ourselves, both as those who may need to continue the ministry and as those who will accompany others through the transition. It is a bit of a macabre joke that "you can't fire a volunteer," which is only true when looked at through the lens of terminating employment! You can invite people to move on from a volunteer ministry—you're not truly "stuck" with people forever, and that sense of helplessness keeps ministry in a death cycle. Certainly, it can be very difficult to gently inform someone that new volunteers will be invited in and that they are being asked to step aside and take on a new role in the community. Some parishes use models to ameliorate that, such as setting "term limits" for volunteer ministries: for example, setting a term of three years for a lector, and then asking the volunteer to step aside and allow others to serve in that role for another three years so as to make space for bringing in new people. Of course, when there is not a boom of volunteers, the idea of removing the standard cadre can feel overwhelming. But it does give a chance for people who might not have felt welcome due to the presence of established volunteers to step up and be invited.

The experience of volunteers moving on is also a really exciting opportunity to cultivate succession planning in volunteer ministries! (I know, who gets that excited about succession planning?) Certainly, a conversation around succession planning should merit way more time than I am able to give here! However, this points back to the burning question of the volunteer who has been serving for thirty-five years that I mentioned earlier: what happens if they move out of the parish, or are too ill to serve, or something tragic happens so that they are no longer volunteering? I am aware of how morbid that question can be for some, but it is a simple fact of life that nothing beyond Christ is permanent. None of us are going to be anywhere forever! Unfortunately, this is how parishes end up in turmoil: when one person is the keeper of the flame, it extinguishes all too easily in their absence. So if someone loves a ministry, surely they want to see it continue long after they are gone—they see the immense value of it and the impact it can have on a community. This is where inviting volunteers to succession planning is an act of love that they can offer for their ministry.

Asking the difficult but important questions ("Who is responsible for this if you are not here?" "What is our one-, three, five-, ten-year plan for this ministry?" "Who do you picture being involved at those points?" "Who are you inviting to be a part of this going forward?") can be strong starts to planning for transition. Consider asking at least the heads of each volunteer ministry—from the annual fish fry to the altar guild and everywhere in between—to invite someone else to be a part of the succession planning. Here is an especially profound opportunity for mentorship and intergenerational ministry to arise organically in parish life: who are volunteers bringing in to mentor, to walk alongside and share their wisdom and expertise in their ministries? Identifying someone else, especially who might be younger than them (great chance to organically involve young adults and young families in parish life!), who they think has the God-given gifts and perhaps a passion for this ministry, is not only a gift for the future but also for those directly involved in the present. For those being mentored, they are identified as potential leaders and celebrated for their gifts, brought to the table even for something as simple as a volunteer ministry; for those doing the mentoring, they are celebrated for their wisdom and able to pass on what they have learned to ensure that what they love lives on. Creating this kind of mentoring/succession planning may require a bit of coaching and accompaniment on your part when you are the priest, but it will pay dividends.

In conclusion, as a priest, as with lay ministry leaders, your ministry will be rife with managing many matters: from finances and buildings to staff and schedules, and so much more. While managing volunteers can feel overwhelming among the many responsibilities, volunteers can be among the greatest assets to a community of faith, and to manage them well lays the foundation for a vibrant parish.

7

Effective Communication Strategies

Helen Osman

Sr. Mary Ann Walsh, a giant in the world of church communications (she was even mentioned by name in at least one edition of the Associated Press's style guide), had lots of memorable lines about the church and its tenuous approach to communications. Bishops and pastors think about communications as a mother would dessert, she'd say. If there was money left over in the budget, or if there was a special event, we could have dessert, or spend money on communications. Otherwise, let's focus on the meat and potatoes of ministry.

She thought that was a terrible way to look at communications. I would agree. Instead of considering communications a nonessential frill, I suggest that parishes (and dioceses) should think of communications as being as essential an element to the church's ministry as vitamins are to a healthy person's daily diet. Without communications, our parish body becomes weak, susceptible to outside diseases, malnourished. Furthermore, the best way to communicate is when it is so integrated into daily programming and processes that it becomes easily consumed and a delight to receive—just as the best way to get one's vitamins is in well-prepared, natural food that tastes delicious.

So how does a parish go about integrating communications into its daily routine? In the parlance of professionals in the field, it's called a *communications strategy*. An effective communications strategy includes at least three elements: (1) a clear vision; (2) specific audiences; and (3) quality content and channels. Another way of describing this is to use the "five Ws" of storytelling: *what* and *why* (vision) do you communicate, *how* (content), and to *whom* and *when* (audiences). This chapter considers each of those three elements, and then provides some tactical means to implement a communications strategy.

A Clear Vision

A parish recently spent a good deal of money to have a big lighted marquee placed on its parish property. This beautiful marker provides a way for the parish to communicate what is important to all who drive by on a busy highway. Sometimes it includes a message about an upcoming event. Sometimes there is a greeting such as "Happy Easter!" But always there are the words, "To rent our parish hall, please call 555-1212." The message is definitely loud and clear: We want your money! Oh, and by the way, here's something that might be meaningful to everyone else. Although that parish expended considerable resources to communicate, it may not have taken the time to be strategic about using that marquee. "What" and "why" were they trying to communicate with that signage?

A vision of communications has to begin with the pastor. When you are a pastor, you will have your own *style* of communication. You may be an introvert or an extrovert. You may be a great preacher or prefer to meet with people one-on-one. You don't need to be all things to all people. But you will need to have a vision for what you want people to think about your parish, how they describe the parish, and what its reputation is.

Our Catholic Church has been doing "visioning" from its very beginning. Who decided that we would call ourselves Christians and Jesus the Christ? The word "Christ" can be translated as "the Anointed One." From the birth of the church, then, our faith ancestors envisioned themselves as "anointed." Perhaps we shouldn't be surprised that the Roman Empire considered them dangerous.

And over the centuries, the church has used symbols—including words—to indicate what it is and what it means to be a member of this church. Fire, for example, is a symbol of the Holy Spirit. Making the sign of the cross marks us. The words "one," "holy," "catholic," and "apostolic" encapsulate the core values of our organization. Companies have become expert at this practice. They call it trademarking, or branding. You need to determine the vision, or the "brand," of your parish—its defining "mark." Is it welcoming? Multicultural? Impressive? Beautiful? Serving? Spiritual?

Some may want to claim all of those as the parish's vision, or brand. While you can certainly make that claim, what happens in reality is either the parish is mediocre in all aspects, or one of these rises to the top in a somewhat organic manner. In other words, the pastor didn't expend enough time and energy to really understand his vision or the lived faith of the parish. You will have to consider your parish's mission statement for clues about what parishioners and the former pastor think its brand should be. You will have to talk with your staff and the parish council. Would they agree with you on the brand, or the defining mark, of the parish?

Once the parish has settled on a brand or trademark, be sure that your staff, pastoral council, and finance council know it and that all of you are working together to strengthen that brand. If your staff and key leadership don't buy into the concept, if they don't "get" the vision, no one else will either.

Specific Audiences

The second part of a communications strategy is understanding key communities. Businesses use the phrases "target audiences" or "key stakeholders" to describe this component. I prefer the word "communities" instead of "audiences" since it suggests a back-and-forth type of communication rather than a one-way street. Dialogue and listening are key attributes of a successful communicator. In his 2014 World Communications Day message, Pope Francis wrote, "The walls which divide us can be broken down only if we are prepared to listen and learn from one another. . . . A culture of encounter demands that we be ready not only to give, but also to receive."[1]

If you are trying to communicate your vision to everyone the same way, you're not going to be successful. You will need to know your communities and what makes each one a community. Some examples could be parents of children in the religious education program and the parish school, liturgical ministers, parish and finance councils, lay organizations, daily Mass attendees, or catechists. In some parishes these are all the same people, but in larger parishes they may have different members.

You will have to consider their unique needs and interests. Do any of them feel ostracized or distanced from the parish leadership, or from one other? Are the parish parents those who work multiple jobs, or are they single parents, stretched for time? Or are there a large number of mothers or fathers who stay home with their children? It will be necessary for you to understand the potential barriers preventing these communities from receiving your parish's communications. You will also need to know what in their lives would resonate with the vision that you have for the parish. For example, if you want your parish to be known as a welcoming parish and you have many single parents, what would help them appreciate that vision? Perhaps providing child care for every event, and communicating that information in a way that encourages parents to utilize the service.

The "when" part of a communications strategy is also about the "who." A joke is not the only communication that benefits from good timing. Many parishes are learning that emails sent on Saturday mornings are opened more often than emails sent on Friday afternoons. Pulpit announcements made at the end of Mass aren't heard by those who leave after Communion. Putting websites (URL links) in printed bulletins requires extra effort from those who may be only mildly interested in reading about an advocacy effort.

While the pastor has to take ownership of setting the vision—the "what" and the "why" of a communications strategy—it will most likely be parishioners who can take the lead in defining the "who" and the "when." Savvy business owners, marketing or fund-raising professionals, or people with experience in sales typically do this work for a living. The diocesan communications, development, or stewardship staff might also be able to help.

While reaching out to your diocese, also ask if it has any communications policies. Most have published, at the very least, basic communications procedures regarding safe environment policies and issues. As you find yourself building your parish communications strategy and training your staff and volunteers, be sure that everything is consistent with diocesan policies.

To reiterate, it will be important that your staff and key parish leadership know the parish's audiences, what their needs are, and the barriers to effectively communicating with them.

Quality Content and Channels

The "how" of a communications strategy tends to get the most attention since it's identified by content and the channels of distribution: in other words, the bulletin, the emails, the website, the signage. Sometimes this is where a pastor or parish staff want to start when they consider communications. Avoid that temptation. Remember Sr. Mary Ann's analogy? If you aren't providing a healthy vision or considering the needs of your communities, no fancy digital app or shining marquee is going to fix anything.

Content should be well written, with high-quality images and well-crafted visual design. The Gospel message deserves our very best work. One way to ensure that is to set up work flows, or processes that allow people with the appropriate skills and authority to make the right decisions. The pastor may have the deepest theological training, but he may write the deadliest run-on sentences ever seen. Let a competent English teacher, journalist, or editor form those sentences into something worthy of Hemingway. They can't alter the theological underpinnings, but they can make it easier for your parishioners to understand what you're trying to communicate.

Deadlines should be realistic and logical. And remember, no matter where you are in the sequencing, if someone misses a deadline, there are consequences down the chain. If you just can't get your column to the bulletin editor until Friday morning, don't be surprised if there are errors in it on Sunday morning.

Honor the medium. Marshall McLuhan famously said, "The medium is the message." There's a lot packed into that phrase, including the notion that you will have to consider the attributes of the media you intend to use when creating content. For instance, a video longer than two minutes is deadly on the web. A beautiful liturgy becomes tedious and tiring when one experiences it on a tiny screen (unless you happen to be the presider's mother). A blog works well on a website, but you may want to include only a sentence or two and a link if you're going to post it on the parish's Facebook page. There are also practical considerations for specific communication channels, which we'll consider below.

Signage and Directions

Is it clear to the uninitiated? A parish we attended always welcomed newcomers to coffee in the St. Francis room. But in all the years I heard that announcement or read it in the bulletin, I never learned where the St. Francis room was. You will have to consider what is most important to people who are trying to navigate your campus for the first time.

Bulletins

These are among the most time-consuming chores for parish staffs, yet most bulletins don't show it. They tend to be a hodgepodge of events and listings of phone numbers. Fortunate are those parishioners who can actually find some *formation* along with *information* inside their parish's bulletin.

In 2012, a study by the Center for Applied Research in the Apostolate (CARA) found that the parish bulletin was by far the most frequently used channel of communication by Catholics to get information about their parish or the church—even among millennials.[2] If less than half of all Catholics read the bulletin, it's still considerably more than the number who access parish websites. So you will have to try to find ways to tell those bulletin readers about the core mission of your parish. Some pastors publish highlights from their homily or their weekly blog posts in the bulletin. Others use content based on the Sunday Scripture that is available from other sources, including the weekly service myUSCCB[3] from the USCCB. It's also possible to provide short news stories about a service project, include some catechesis in the announcement about the upcoming confirmations, or provide a "teaser" to entice people to go to your website or to read a really interesting article in the diocesan newspaper.

But what about all those event announcements that someone (often the parish secretary) says absolutely must be included? That information must get out to parishioners, but taking up valuable "real estate" inside a parish bulletin may not be the best way to reach people. Consider emailing those announcements to parishioners so that everyone, regardless of whether they attend Sunday Mass, receives the information. In that way the bulletin—replete with more *formation* content—becomes a valid communications channel that enhances the experience of those who have attended Mass.

Email

Marketers tell us that we've come full circle in the world of digital marketing. After trying out advertising on websites, then Facebook, Pinterest, YouTube, and other social media channels, they're discovering that emails are the most effective way to reach people.

Parishes are no different. One pastor told me his staff reports an 80 to 90 percent open rate on the emails sent to parishioners. "Open rate" tells us how many emails were actually clicked on and "opened" by recipients. Most software programs that provide email management can give this kind of information. Using email management software also ensures that emails aren't being blocked by spam filters and that you can monitor "bouncebacks." Some companies that offer website or data-management solutions also provide email management. It's worth the investment.

Websites

Many websites have the same feel as parish bulletins: they look like someone opened a box of trinkets and scattered them around. So many shiny jewels, it's hard to decide which one to select. Others require you to click not once, not twice, but maybe three or four times before you find out the Mass schedule or where the parish is located.

A service such as Google Analytics can help you discover *how* people use your website. As a general rule, though, it should serve two purposes.

First, it should be a digital "welcoming kit" for people interested in what the parish provides, such as the sacraments and a sense of community. Typically, the first place people go when searching for anything is the internet. The Barna Group, which does research for churches, nonprofits, and businesses, found in a 2013 study on practicing millennials (18- to 30-year-olds) that 56 percent check out a parish's website before visiting the church.

You will have to be sure your site is built in a way that search engines can find it. If you don't know what that means, find a company that does and pay them to host the site and provide you with a content-management system that will allow your staff to update content on a regular basis. Don't let your website grow into a monstrosity of pages and broken links. If you want to archive the content, create a separate digital space. And it should be the job of someone other than the pastor to maintain editorial and operational oversight of that content. It could be a parish staff member or an experienced volunteer or team.

Second, consider the website a source of *great* content about the parish. Post photo galleries and short stories or blogs. Then repurpose that content by sharing it on the parish's social media. Again, think about those "seekers" who are looking on the internet for a faith home. What aspect of your parish's vision would entice them to come to Mass this Sunday?

If your future parish is large, or has good funding, consider software that allows integration of email management with a website system. Software that accomplishes this is often known as a membership or association management system. There are even companies that market systems specifically to Catholic parishes, but many parishes use membership management systems that service not only churches but also universities, professional organizations, and fraternal organizations. These systems can also record and accept donations as well as registrations and payments for religious education and other programming.

Social Media

Social media is a source of great angst and consternation for most pastors. Anecdotally, I see less hand-wringing as a younger generation of digitally savvy men move into rectories, but there are still parishes with policies that do not allow staff or priests to post anything about the parish on social media. This is unfortunate, since these restrictive parishes are making themselves invisible to a growing number of young Catholics. They are isolating their community from a world that is embracing new technology.

Pope Benedict was the first pope to encourage the church to move into this new world. In fact, he coined a phrase for it: the "digital continent." In 2009, he wrote, "These technologies are truly a gift to humanity and we must endeavor to ensure that the benefits they offer are put at the service of all human individuals and communities, especially those who are most disadvantaged and vulnerable."[4] To understand the philosophy of the Holy Father and the Holy See regarding the new media, take time to read the World Communications Day messages. These have been issued annually since 1967, but if you are pressed for time, start with the message for 2007.[5] If you feel like a Luddite and are incapable of understanding young people and their odd jargon, these messages provide a strong pastoral rationale for why it's important for your parish to use such channels as Facebook and YouTube. Pope Francis summed up the Vatican's vision well: "The internet, in particular, offers immense possibilities for encounter and solidarity. This is something truly good, a gift from God."[6]

There are good reasons, of course, why parishes are leery of social media. It has a dark side and the medium is not for the uninitiated. The USCCB provides a set of guidelines that are extremely useful and necessary to read, even for parishes already using social media. The guidelines provide definitions of terms, best practices, how to administer social media sets, how to use social networks with minors, what to say to staff about personal sites, and how to report and monitor.[7]

Video, Audio, and More

Some parishes maintain a much larger arsenal of communications channels: a televised Mass, for example, or a low-power AM station, or a bookstore. Each of these has attributes that should be leveraged as much as possible, but that's a conversation beyond the scope of this chapter. Suffice it to say that caution is warranted in each case: if the content doesn't serve the vision of the pastor or the needs of the community, there will not be sufficient return on investment.

Media Relations

This is another area pastors often wish would disappear. Indeed, when a reporter calls it's not usually because something marvelous just happened at the parish. The best advice here is to be sure that whoever answers the parish phone knows how to respond to a reporter's call, particularly who to hand it off to. This is an area in which you will absolutely want to be sure you're in alignment with diocesan guidelines. Pastors and parish staff can take comfort in the fact the diocesan communications director usually prefers that he or she talk to the reporter.

Crisis communication plans should be integrated into the parish's overall crisis plans. You should not wait for a natural disaster or a human tragedy to strike to begin finding essential phone numbers or figuring out how to send out email blasts. In these events, the secular media—especially radio, television, and social media—can be your best ally in getting the word out quickly.

Sometimes overlooked among the thicket of information outlets today is the diocesan communication channel. Parishioners may already receive the diocesan newspaper. It's not unreasonable to conclude that its content, or content on the diocesan website and social media that aligns with your parishioners' needs or interests, could supplement the parish's own content and be leveraged to bring people to the parish, either in person or via its communications channels. Theology on Tap, for instance, is a program geared toward young Catholics who may be seeking a parish home. You could follow the diocesan social media channels that promote Theology on Tap events, and then provide posts that inform young people about your parish's events that might be of interest to them.

As a final thought, the words "communications," "community," and "communion" share a common root. As Pope Francis wrote in the 2014 World Communications Day message, "Good communication helps us to grow closer, to know one another better, and ultimately, to grow in unity."

Our desire for communion should compel us to be not just good communicators, but *Gospel-good* communicators. Our community deserves nothing less.

Endnotes

1. Message of Pope Francis for the 48th World Communications Day, "Communication at the Service of an Authentic Culture of Encounter," June 1, 2014, https://w2.vatican.va/content/francesco/en/messages/communications/documents/papa-francesco_20140124_messaggio-comunicazioni-sociali.html.

2. Mark Gray and Mary Gautier, *Catholic New Media Use in the United States, 2012* (Washington, DC: Center for Applied Research in the Apostolate [CARA]).

3. For myUSCCB, go to https://usccb.my.site.com/login and click "Sign Up."

4. Message of the Holy Father Benedict XVI for the 43rd World Communications Day, "New Technologies, New Relationships: Promoting a Culture of Respect, Dialogue and Friendship," May 24, 2009, https://www.vatican.va/content/benedict-xvi/en/messages/communications/documents/hf_ben-xvi_mes_20090124_43rd-world-communications-day.html.

5. Message of the Holy Father Benedict XVI for the 41st World Communications Day, "Children and the Media: A Challenge for Education," May 20, 2007, https://www.vatican.va/content/benedict-xvi/en/messages/communications/documents/hf_ben-xvi_mes_20070124_41st-world-communications-day.html.

6. Message of Francis for 48th World Communications Day.

7. USCCB, "Social Media Guidelines," https://www.usccb.org/committees/communications/social-media-guidelines.

Tools for Leadership: Feedback and Development Plans

Michael Brough

In over twenty years of working with and training priests in a dozen different countries around the world, what's impressed me the most is how all of you want to be the best priest, the best pastor, the best leader possible for the people you serve. At the Leadership Roundtable, we've learned a great deal about how to develop leaders—lay and ordained—in the Catholic Church. And my goal is to impart to you some of those insights to help better prepare you for your challenging role as pastor.

Let's start with a brief introduction to the leadership role of a pastor. When you become a pastor, you are a leader, but who do you lead? What do you lead? What formation have you received in preparation for that leadership role? To help answer those questions, we're going to look at three different aspects of leadership for the ministry, and the essential tools for developing those competencies. We're going to focus on leading yourself, leading others, and leading the organization. Those, in sum, are what parish leadership is about.

For all of us as Catholic leaders, a model of perfect servant leadership exists in John 13:1-15, where Jesus washes the feet of his disciples. In our own ministry, we are called to grow in the likeness of Jesus so that we can more accurately reflect his life and communicate his message. We understand we can only appreciate and truly understand the meaning of that leadership and ministry as we exercise it, and as we reflect upon both our words and our actions. We had a great reminder from our Holy Father Pope Francis as he began his Petrine ministry, counseling us that "authentic power is service."

It's important for us to always look at our pastoral leadership in terms of a spirituality of leadership. I once heard it said that leaders of a community need to be able to *organize* its members, *animate* it to make it alive, and *love* each person for their personal growth in order to be most effective.

So, organize, animate, and love: three elements of our pastoral leadership ministry. Priests have told us over the years that some of those leadership skills have been taught to them better than others. Some they've learned in the seminary, some from experienced priests and lay leaders, and some through ministry situations in the parish. The four tools offered in this chapter are designed specifically to help develop those leadership skills that will be required of you as pastor of a parish. To reinforce them, I'm going to share with you some lessons we've learned at the Leadership Roundtable through a project we developed called Catholic Leadership 360 (www.leadershiproundtable.org/drawer/catholic-leadership-360). It's a unique collaboration with the National Federation of Priests' Councils and the National Association of Church Personnel Administrators to develop leaders, both lay and ordained, within the church. We also benefited from the research and educational products of the Center for Creative Leadership (www.CCL.org), which informs the four tools offered in this chapter.

Assessing the Need for Leadership Development

We'll begin our discussion of leadership development with a number of questions that I'm sure have arisen within your own ministry. How do you know how well you're doing as a leader? How can new pastors learn how to become good pastors? How can you tell your leadership strengths and development needs? And how do we encourage accountability for the ongoing formation of priests?

Fortunately, the USCCB addressed these issues in their 1984 document on the need for the continuing formation of priests. They described it as "a lifelong dialog journey through which a priest comes to greater awareness of one's self, others, and God. Personal growth, continuing formation, theological education, and human development. All of which lead to greater service of the people of God. These are woven throughout the priest's entire life and ministry."

The bishops were even more explicit in their 2005 document *Co-Workers in the Vineyard of the Lord*. Here, they speak of the need for evaluation and feedback for those of us in ministry, for formal written appraisals within the context of our mission (in this case as pastor), and for recognizing that we have both deficiencies we need to work on and strengths that need to be recognized and developed or leveraged. *Co-Workers* states,

> In a comprehensive personnel system, this area [evaluation and feedback] addresses regular performance appraisals, as a part of ministerial workplace practice, that provide a formal opportunity for every individual minister to reflect on his or her own performance and get feedback from a supervisor and that may include the views of colleagues and those served. Appraisal and feedback is most effective when conducted in the context of the mission of the parish or diocese. Documentation of honest and constructive feedback about deficiencies and subsequent steps for improvement is important, as is both formal and informal recognition of generous, Christ-centered, and effective service.[1]

With that as backdrop, here are some specific lessons we've learned working with priests:

First, we need leadership development that creates adaptive solutions. We don't learn how to be leaders for a fixed situation. We're faced with changing conditions, unexpected happenings, and new people coming into the situation.

Second, we need leadership development that expands the leadership space. That means involving others in leadership. It means using and developing persuasive skills for working with others. It means being respectful, building trust between those we lead and ourselves.

Third, we need to develop reflective leaders. Priests are particularly good at this. It's part of the formation that we go through as Catholic ministry leaders—where solutions emerge from prayer, discernment, and dialogue. Solutions emerge over time with reflection.

Fourth, we need help on how to identify priorities. This is perhaps the biggest challenge many pastors face. How do we identify our priorities? How do we manage our time? How do we make sure that we are accessible to people? How do we use our time in both formal and informal settings within the parish?

And finally, we need leadership development that is responsible to the church, that reflects the values and beliefs of the church, and that is open to a broader understanding of who we are as the church and what it means to be *church*.

Perhaps the most important lesson we've learned is that for development to really work it requires three different components: assessment, challenge, and support. If you put those three elements together, then you have a better chance of growth. But in our work with pastors and priests we've come to realize that for leadership development to really work well it must be within the broader context of diocese and ministry. In other words, I recognize that my leadership development is not simply something I do alone, but that other priests are going through that same development at the same time as part of a broader, shared mission, and that there are ways for us to connect and to support one another in that process.

Having said that, let's take a look at four essential leadership development tools pastors should have in their toolbox.

Tool One: Identify Competencies

What do I mean by leadership competencies? Our partners at the Center for Creative Leadership describe competencies as measurable characteristics of a person that are related to success at work. A competency may be a behavioral skill such as acting fairly, not playing favorites. It could be a technical skill such as public speaking. It could be an attribute such as intelligence or it could be an attitude such as optimism.

There are literally hundreds of leadership competencies. What we've done at the Leadership Roundtable, and in the Catholic Leadership 360 program, is select thirteen pastoral leadership competencies from three different sources: *Pastores Dabo Vobis* (1992), the *Basic Plan for the Ongoing Formation of Priests* (2001), and *In Fulfillment of Their Mission* (2008), a document on the duty and tasks of Roman Catholic priests. These cover a broad range of competencies required of a priest, such as communicating ideas and information, inspiring commitment from others, bringing out the best in people, forging synergy, developing relationships, having respect for differences between individuals and groups, and selecting and developing people to work within ministry. They also include competencies like courage, openness, and flexibility, as well as a willingness to learn and a commitment to personal ongoing formation. These competencies are combined with specific ministerial competencies that relate to your identity and your role as pastor and priest. In other words, how will you be most effective in your priestly ministry?

Let's take a closer look at one of those competencies: How effective are you in communicating ideas and information? And to that end, what are the specific behaviors and skills you will require as pastor? Some are written communication skills, while others are verbal capabilities that help determine how well you impart ideas and vision in a parish council meeting, for example. Another example of a competency is being able to overcome resistance that sometimes occurs when you're trying to communicate a particular message.

Tool Two: Gather Feedback

As leadership guru Ann Morrison reminds us in *Breaking the Glass Ceiling*, "While perceptions may not be the ultimate truth, they are what people use to make decisions."[2] So, gathering feedback is important. Understanding how you are perceived as a leader is important. Of course, you will get feedback informally from people all the time in the parish. But how can you get formal feedback that will help you to develop leadership competencies—the leadership skills—that you require as pastor? Let's consider four relevant questions:

First, who should you ask for feedback? The best sort of feedback is 360-degree feedback. As the name suggests, that means not just from one person, like your boss or someone you work with or a direct-report or someone you serve, but rather from *all* of these. Ask for feedback from people who know you and the role you're being asked to play, and who are willing to give an honest answer so that you can learn and grow from it. Identify as many people as possible who may be in a position to offer you their perceptions. The more feedback you receive, the more you can remove layers of subjectivity and arrive at bigger-picture conclusions.

Second, when is a good time to ask for feedback? The answer, of course, is constantly, so that you can get feedback on a regular basis and see the results of adjustments you're making. But it's very important to ask for feedback when there is a specific competency or leadership-development skill that you're looking to focus on and improve. If I've received feedback that says, "Michael, you really could work on your communication skills," then it's good for me to ask people, "Okay, let's talk about which communication skills I need to improve, and can you give me feedback on them?"

Third, how should you ask for feedback? In addition to the generalities that informal feedback tends to produce, it's important to collect some formal feedback. That means asking people directly, "Can you describe for me the specific *situation* in which you've observed this behavior?" "What specific *behaviors* did you observe?" "And can you tell me the *impact* that behavior had?" That allows you to know as a person trying to develop your leadership skills what you need to focus on. It's important to note that we're not talking here about personality-driven leadership. Some people like our style, others don't. Some people like our personality, others don't. That's not what we're talking about developing here. We're talking instead about getting feedback on specific behaviors—because behaviors we can change. Personality we're stuck with!

Fourth, how should you use the feedback you receive? Focus on the future, not the past. The feedback will by definition refer to past events, but how can you use the information to change future encounters? Some of the best advice here is to focus on one particular competency you've received feedback on and ask yourself, "How am I going to improve in this area?" If you're dedicated to making a change and acknowledging that this is the behavior you want to work on, then you can make a difference. The other way to use feedback is to evaluate it carefully, since not all feedback is equal. Which leads us to the question: How do you interpret feedback? Well, you know what it's like at the end of Sunday Mass when everyone walks past the priest and shakes his hand. "Great sermon, Father," someone says, but the next ten walk past and don't reference the sermon at all. So, is that helpful feedback? Is it just one person who thought it was a great sermon, or is it that the others didn't take the time to tell the priest? Or did the others think it was merely average, or maybe terrible and they're not coming back? So informal feedback is fine, but it's not nearly as helpful as getting ongoing formal feedback from people. One small piece of feedback is not the whole picture. It's a snapshot. It gives you a useful piece of information, but then you need to interpret the data.

I've seen two common mistakes in terms of how people interpret feedback. The first is that they agree too quickly. "Oh yes, that's me alright; not much I can do about it." The second is that they disagree too quickly. "That's not true. That's not who I am." Both reactions are counterproductive. It's important to take time to reflect upon the feedback you've received—particularly if it's focused feedback—and decide how you're going to respond.

Tool Three: Create a Development Plan

Don't panic. This isn't as complicated as it might sound, especially if you follow these four steps:

First, identify your strengths and development needs. You can understand these in four different ways. One way is your confirmed strengths, where you receive feedback that says, "Okay, you're really good at this." You always thought you were, so this is now a confirmed strength. Then there are unrecognized strengths, areas you didn't know you were good at but where people said through their feedback, "Yes, this is how you come across. This is how we experience your leadership." The third way is confirmed development needs: somebody gives you feedback that suggests "You need to work on this," and you acknowledge, "Yes, this is an area I know from past experience I need to work on." And fourth is unrecognized development needs. These are the blind spots—areas you didn't realize you needed help with until feedback alerted you to your shortcomings.

Second, create a development plan to prioritize the feedback you receive. In other words, how important is this feedback for your ministry? Yes, you'd like to develop this or that skill, but is it really important to you at this time? Looking ahead, what challenges will you face in your pastoral leadership over the next year or two? Obviously, if you can develop a skill you know you're going to need, that will allow you to meet those challenges more effectively. And two final questions in terms of prioritizing feedback: Is it worth the time and effort it will take to make changes in this area, and how motivated are you to undertake those changes? Frankly, this requires you to be very honest with yourself because if you don't have the motivation—even if it's an area that needs development—it's probably best to choose another area where you're more likely to be successful. As a rule of thumb, as long as your weaknesses are not derailments (i.e., as long as they do not stop you from being effective in your ministry), it is more worthwhile to further develop your strengths.

Third, identify and articulate your goals. Let's be clear here—we're not talking about a five-page document listing a whole bunch of goals. I'm suggesting instead that two or three development goals at any one time are sufficient. My experience in working with and coaching others is that if you identify one goal to focus on and prove to be successful with it, then you're more likely to come back to goals two and three and try to develop them. Don't overreach. Choosing goals that are important to you and that you can commit to accomplishing is the best formula for success. As with any goals, of course, they should be clear, specific, and assessable. And there should be a time frame for completing them, along with specific action steps: "This is what I'm going to do. These are the behaviors I'm going to change." And finally, be clear about the outcomes. In other words, "I expect within the time frame I've set to be able to accomplish this or that." If you don't set clear outcomes, you'll never know if you've achieved your goals.

Fourth and finally, make sure you follow through. This, unfortunately, is often neglected, leading to tremendous frustration. It's pointless to go through the process of getting feedback, identifying competencies to improve, and creating goals if you don't intend to follow through. This means not just responding to feedback you've already received, but responding to feedback you *continue* to receive. Holding yourself accountable is the key here. Best practice calls for sharing your development goals with others to help you hold yourself accountable, as well as to solicit their help and support. Set a specific time to review whether or not you've achieved your goals. This may involve meeting with a supervisor, superior, coach, or friend—someone who will hold you accountable. In the end, this is a very adult model for learning and for ensuring leadership development.

To help firm up for you what I mean by setting concrete goals, here's an example I've adapted from feedback specialists Karen Kirkland and Sam Manoogian in their practical guidebook, *Ongoing Feedback*:

> I will improve my effectiveness in leading my pastoral team by concentrating on the following two goals. I will learn to reserve judgment on others' ideas by making sure that my initial response is not a negative one. Additionally, I will ask for input from the group before decisions are made or finalized. I will ask Deacon Jose, a friend and mentor, to give me feedback and help me monitor my progress. I will achieve these goals by July 1st, six months from now.[3]

You can see in these goals the infrastructure of a sound development plan:

- Here's the behavior I'm going to change.
- Here are the specific goals to make that happen.
- Here's how I plan to get feedback and monitor my progress.
- Here's the timeline I've set.

Tool Four: Engage Support/Identify a Coach

You are more likely to be successful developing your leadership skills if you create developmental relationships. These relationships fulfill three essential functions: *assessment*—helping you assess your performance on a continuing basis; *challenge*—pushing you beyond your normal comfort zone; and *support*—providing both ministry and personal support.

One of the most effective forms of support in working with priests and bishops—something that's observable in the secular realm as well—is a coach. Coaching is defined as helping, motivating, enabling people—professionally and/or personally—to determine a direction and move swiftly toward their goals. Indeed, it's about helping people transition from where they are to where they want to be. A coach can be invaluable in helping you grow your competence, commitment, and confidence. He or she can make the difference between a leadership development plan that succeeds, and one that fails.[4]

Reflecting on the Journey Ahead

In concluding this chapter on leadership development, here are some questions to reflect on:

- What have you learned about leading yourself?
- What have you learned about leading others?
- What have you learned about leading your organization?
- What leadership competency can you commit yourself to work on and improve?
- What further assistance do you need in order to be able to develop these skills?

As you focus on the commitment you've made to your ongoing formation and development, you have my hopes and prayers, as well as those of your parishioners, that you may continue to develop the requisite skills and become leaders as fathers, as brothers, and as companions on the journey of faith. As our Holy Father Pope Francis put it, speaking to male religious in November 2013,

> In life it is difficult for everything to be clear, precise, outlined neatly. . . . Life is complicated; it consists of grace and sin. . . . We all make mistakes and we need to recognize our weaknesses. . . . We always must think of the people of God in all of this. Just think of reli-

gious who have hearts that are as sour as vinegar: they are not made for the people. In the end we must not form administrators, managers, but fathers, brothers, traveling companions.[5]

Endnotes

1. USCCB, *Co-Workers in the Vineyard of the Lord: A Resource for Guiding the Development of Lay Ecclesial Ministry* (Washington, DC: USCCB, 2005).

2. Ann M. Morrison, Randall P. White, Ellen Van Velsor, and the Center for Creative Leadership, *Breaking the Glass Ceiling: Can Women Reach the Top of America's Largest Corporations?*, updated ed. (New York: Perseus, 1992), 24.

3. Karen Kirkland and Sam Manoogian, *Ongoing Feedback: How to Get It, How to Use It* (Greensboro, NC: Center for Creative Leadership, 2004).

4. For further resources to help you achieve your development goals, visit www.leadershiproundtable.org/drawer/catholic-leadership-360.

5. Joshua McElwee, "Pope Calls Religious to Be 'Real Witnesses,'" *National Catholic Reporter*, January 14, 2014.

9

Leading Effective Meetings

Peter Denio

A colleague of mine who is a pastoral associate in a suburban parish tells of the time he passed a parishioner in the hallway of the parish center. The individual offhandedly remarked, "I have the pastoral council meeting tonight, but I hate going. It's such a waste of time." After the encounter, the pastoral associate thought about how unfortunate it was to have a dedicated parishioner feel that his time and gifts were being wasted at what should be such an important gathering for the parish. Later that same day, the pastoral associate crossed paths with the pastor of the parish. As they stopped to discuss a few items of business, the memory of the exchange with the parishioner was still fresh in the associate's mind. He contemplated bringing it up, but before he could the pastor ventured, "Tonight's the pastoral council meeting, and I dread going. It feels like we never accomplish anything."

I'm sure you've been there. We all have! Maybe not specifically with regard to a pastoral council you have been part of, but other groups and meetings that have prompted similar thoughts. For all the bad raps they take, though, meetings are necessary. Effective meetings can help the parish move toward a common vision articulated by the pastor and pastoral council. They can advance creative solutions to difficult and challenging pastoral problems. On the other hand, meetings all too often turn into unproductive—even detrimental—exchanges between participants, convinced their time was ill spent. Such sentiments over time can lead people to feel frustrated, burnt out, apathetic, or even helpless. And I submit that ineffective meetings can contribute to the stagnation of parish life and are a major cause of "maintenance mentality" in a majority of parishes, where the same activity is done year after year without attempting to link it to a broader vision of where the parish is headed or what should be changed to meet new pastoral challenges.

When you are a pastor, you will come to know that meetings run the gamut from sit-downs with pre-Cana couples to staff meetings to sessions with individuals for pastoral care or counseling, and from parish plenary sessions to diocesan committee meetings to small Christian community or prayer groups—sometimes all in one day! My goal is to identify some key principles and structures that can help pastoral leaders run tighter and more productive parish meetings. And in so doing, I'd like to focus on meetings that directly impact the goals and vision of the parish. These typically involve the parish pastoral staff, finance and pastoral councils, stewardship committee, and other ministry leadership teams.

Where Should I Spend My Limited Time?

When you become a pastor you will become familiar with delegating responsibilities to parish bodies that work with you toward a common vision for the parish. You will also spend time ministering and interacting with those you serve. But to what degree do you give—and should you give—to each?

The simple answer is you need to strike a balance. You may find yourself doing 80 percent direct ministry and 20 percent collaboration with parish leadership bodies and ministry leaders. If you're in the process of taking the parish toward new goals propelled by a bold new vision, then your time should probably be weighted more toward working with leadership bodies. This isn't to say that all parishioners shouldn't have access to you. But if you find it hard to focus on strategic leadership decisions required of you, then it's time to take a second look at how you're allocating your time. True, you may be the only priest in the parish, or you may find a dearth of leadership talent around you. In these cases, however, the onus is even greater to transition responsibilities that don't require your gifts or authority as pastor to someone else. One "best practice" is to have two volunteer coleaders for all parish leadership positions to ensure continuity, stability, and succession.

Is This Meeting Necessary (and if So, Do I Need to Be There)?

"Father, can I meet with you?" Even if you've grown weary of hearing that request, you need to take it seriously. The reason is clear: if you make yourself inaccessible to people in leadership roles, you run the risk of stifling the flow of information and ideas essential to creative problem solving and building a parish focused on the future.

The converse is also true. As pastor you may be invited or, if parish responsibilities are not clearly delegated, *required* to attend meetings where your presence isn't really essential. One way to excise these expendable meetings from your pastoral life is to pose a couple of fundamental questions: (1) What is the purpose of the meeting? and (2) Do I really need to be the one attending?

If the meeting has anything to do with the parish's longer range goals and vision, or with an urgent pending matter, then you probably should be present. If, on the other hand, you determine your presence is not required, you should consider delegating the responsibility to a staff or council member or parishioner. Here are some additional questions to help with that decision:

- Am I comfortable delegating responsibility to someone else?
- If I delegate, does the person have the information needed to present the item at the meeting, or do I need to spend time now or later preparing and updating them?
- Is there any information that can be sent to participants ahead of the meeting that might allow for a more informed conversation?

Remember, too, there are times when you will simply have to postpone a meeting due to greater priorities on your plate, or because your own personal obligations or wellness demand it. As pastor, you will have the prerogative to make that call.

How to Avoid "Meeting Soup"

Patrick Lencioni, a business-management consultant and Catholic layman who has donated considerable time to advising church leadership, describes how parish meetings often devolve into what he calls "meeting soup"—brimming with a hodgepodge of agenda items that are often unrelated and have varying levels of importance. For example, the replacement of folding tables and chairs for the parish recreation room may compete on the agenda with development of a program designed to lead parishioners to a greater role in evangelization. This can easily happen when there is a lack of understanding and agreement over the parish's priorities and how to structure effective meetings around them. Just as importantly, a way must be found to match attendees to the appropriate agenda items so that individuals are not wasting their time on matters unrelated to their parish roles and responsibilities.

Keeping Your Meetings Priority Driven

To avoid getting mired in "meeting soup," key leadership (pastoral staff, pastoral and finance council members) must have a clear understanding of the most important priority for the parish. With this as a baseline, it becomes much easier to set the agenda for targeted leadership meetings with the right people attending. I can't emphasize it enough: knowing the parish's priority is the greatest imperative for effective meetings.

How does a parish identify this priority? The pastor in consultation with the parish staff and councils, and sometimes other key groups, needs to take the lead. The priority should be set every one to three years. That's long enough to give the parish time to make substantial progress toward its vision, but short enough to create a sense of urgency.

For example, let's say a parish decides to adopt the *field hospital image of church*, as called for by Pope Francis, as its top priority over the next two to three years. As it moves toward that goal, the following criteria are important:

1. It is tightly focused on a *single priority*: becoming a *field hospital*.

2. Its work is *qualitative*: the experience of the ministries and activities will be evaluated on how well they live up to the vision of being a field hospital.

3. The job is *time-bound*: two to three years.

4. The goal is *affirmed and shared* by all in pastoral leadership. It cannot only be the pastor's vision; all those in leadership should assent and commit to it.

With this priority set, the pastor, staff, and key ministry leaders can enter into their yearly pastoral planning meeting (typically off-site; see below under meeting types) by identifying and discussing the three to five strategies best suited to lead them toward that vision for their church. A highly functioning organization with sufficient staff and resources can probably handle up to eight strategies. Parishes stretched for talent, time, and resources, however, would be well advised to start out with fewer strategies and increase them over time.

The following three strategies might emerge at that pastoral planning meeting on the road to becoming a *field hospital* for the parish and community:

1. Identify and respond to the greatest pastoral needs (physical, social, and spiritual) in their community.
2. Emphasize the healing sacraments of reconciliation and the anointing of the sick throughout parish activities wherever possible.
3. Increase attention to and care for the pastoral needs—physical, social, and spiritual—of those involved in sacramental preparation within the parish (First Eucharist, confirmation, RCIA, marriage preparation).

To repeat, it's critical to identify the parish's top priority and strategies. Only then can all pastoral leadership teams and councils structure their meetings with clarity.

Select the Most Appropriate Type of Meeting

In the following chart, management expert Patrick Lencioni describes the various types of parish meetings tailored to specific needs, along with their formats.[1]

Meeting Type	Time Required	Purpose / Format	Keys to Success
Daily check-in	5–10 minutes	Share daily schedules and activities	• Don't sit down • Keep it administrative • Don't cancel
Weekly or bimonthly staff meeting	45–90 minutes	Review weekly activities and metrics and resolve tactical obstacles and issues	• Don't set agenda until after initial reporting • Postpone strategic discussions
Ad hoc topical	2–4 hours	Discuss, analyze, brainstorm, and decide upon critical issues affecting long-term plans	• Limit to 1–2 topics • Prepare and do research ahead of meeting • Engage in good conflict
Quarterly/off-site	1–2 days	Review strategy, landscape, trends, key personnel, team development	• Get out of parish office • Focus on work; limit social activities • Don't overstructure or overburden schedule

The Daily Check-In

A seldom-used approach to parish meetings with the potential to significantly upgrade communications is known as the daily check-in. Part of the challenge today is that ministry happens round the clock. Pastoral and administrative staffs, along with volunteers, are engaged at different and diverse times of the day and week, often resulting in miscommunication or absence of communication and collaboration.

Daily check-ins should be timed to coincide with periods of the day and week when most key ministerial and administrative leaders are present at the parish. Those might be right after daily Mass, for example, or just before lunch, or thirty minutes before the close of the parish office for the day. Experiment and explore what works best for your parish. Ideally, you should block out one time, or in some cases two times, a day for these five-to-ten-minute on-your-feet check-ins. It's my experience that so much more can be accomplished when people know there's a reserved time during which they're likely to connect with people they need to talk to. As Lencioni emphasizes, these meetings should be no longer than ten minutes—a rule that should be strictly enforced. Within this format, quick questions, updates, and scheduling matters can be effectively dispatched. Some of the greatest benefits will accrue to pastors, who will begin to see fewer interruptions in their daily schedules. The other good news is that if someone misses a check-in meeting, another is only twenty-four hours away.

The Weekly or Bimonthly Staff Meeting

This is probably the most common type of parish meeting, important because it provides an opportunity for the staff to stay informed about progress on priorities identified by the parish. Just as importantly, it ensures that the pastor and other key leaders are privy to the conversations and information essential to moving the parish toward its goals.

The weekly or bimonthly staff meeting serves as a problem-solving space. Ideally, information is provided to participants ahead of time, which requires some advance reading and preparation. That feature, in turn, helps to ensure wise and productive use of time when the meeting takes place. Indeed, individuals are more likely to become engaged with an issue, challenge, or matter of concern to the parish when they've already made an investment in its solution.

Be advised that the staff meeting—like each of the other meeting types—has a standard duration that should be obeyed. If a matter can't be resolved within that time frame, then an *ad hoc meeting* (see meeting types below) should be scheduled, rather than taxing everyone's patience and brain cells by dragging it out.

For maximum effectiveness, the forty-five-to-ninety-minute weekly or bimonthly staff meeting should include the following elements:

Faith sharing. An essential aspect of any parish meeting, particularly those that involve key parish leadership, is faith sharing. This is different from the *read prayer* or *rote prayer* done in unison. It's a time where group members reflect together on their lives informed by faith. A version of the *lectio divina* prayer style is perfect for this meditation, or for other forms of faith sharing that purposely connect our lives to our faith. Why is this so important?

- It grounds the conversation and deliberations that follow to our relationship with God. Intentionally inviting the Holy Spirit into our minds and hearts changes us and has the power to change our conversations. We are able to do more, and do it based on the will of God (instead of our own will), when we spend time listening to what God has to say to us *first* instead of us speaking first or, perhaps even worse, not listening at all.

- It strengthens the bond within the leadership community. Paul's image of us as the Body of Christ can only be true if we work at making it reality. We need to understand the "joys and hopes, the grief and anguish" (*Gaudium et Spes* 1)[2] of each other if we are truly to live as St. Paul taught, so "that there may be no dissension within the body, but the members may have the same care for one another" (1 Cor 12:25).

- The reflection is valuable to all preachers of the parish whose responsibility it is to tend to what is happening in the parish and the wider society.[3]

A "lightning round." The next few minutes of the staff meeting should be used for brief updates on matters that can be resolved through a simple yes-or-no answer or an on-the-spot administrative decision. If the matter is more complex—say two ministry leaders need to connect about an upcoming night of reflection during Lent, or information needs to be passed from one staff member to another regarding a conversation with a parishioner after Mass—then time should be set aside following the meeting to discuss it in greater detail. The overarching goal of this phase of the meeting is brevity, and the facilitator (and ideally all members at the meeting) needs to hold participants accountable.

Developing a "scoreboard." According to Lencioni's formula for good meetings, the agenda should be set *after* the lightning round. That's correct—the agenda should not be created ahead of the meeting! This may sound counterintuitive, but the truth is your leadership agenda should in effect already exist: *It's the priority and strategies previously identified by the parish.* In the example above, the agenda is to become a *field hospital* for the parish and the community, and to that end three concrete strategies were identified. Without clarity on where the parish is going (its vision) or how leadership plans to get there (its strategies), leadership meetings can meander between competing priorities among participants. With a vision and strategies in place, however, the pathway is clear for a productive session.

Lencioni's "scoreboard" is a great way to actually nail down the agenda. The process starts by identifying each strategy and rating it with a color code, as follows:

- *Green* if progress is being made according to plan.
- *Yellow* if there is some delay or challenge, but work is still proceeding.
- *Red* if the item could benefit from group discussion and problem solving.

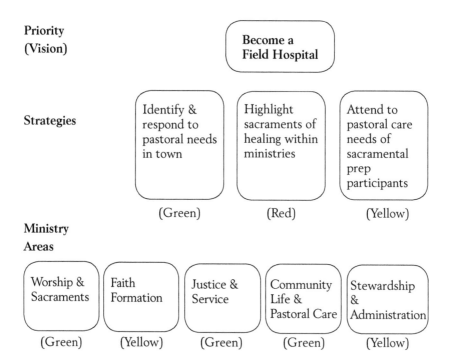

The agenda for the meeting thus becomes any strategy identified as red. Green strategies never make it to the table because they are going according to the plan. Yellow strategies become simply an update, so participants are aware of any delay.

The beauty of this approach is manifold: (1) It focuses members on what they have determined is the group's priority for the parish; (2) it eliminates ancillary topics that sometimes find their way into agendas when they don't really belong there; (3) it keeps the focus of the meeting on problem solving (as it should be at a leadership meeting) and not on reporting; and (4) items that have been identified as important but not in need of problem solving are not discussed, freeing up meeting time for more pressing matters facing the parish.

The facilitator of the meeting can be anyone on the team, or the job can rotate among staff members. I have seen meetings where the pastor or the pastoral or finance council chair served quite successfully in that role. A standardized process for identifying the agenda alleviates the burden on the facilitator. This allows the facilitator to focus on his or her primary responsibilities of ensuring (1) all viewpoints are raised and discussed; (2) a decision or action is identified by the close of the conversation; and (3) there is clarity on the agreed-upon decision or action and commitment by the participants to execute it.

Each strategy has a designated monitor. At the meeting, when the scoreboard is being reviewed in order to create the agenda, each monitor is asked to identify progress on their strategy using the color-coded system. The monitor is not the person who is solely responsible for seeing the strategy through—that rests with the entire leadership team (and likely others within the parish). Instead, the monitor is charged with being aware of and reporting on progress relevant to the strategy. Color-coding, for its part, is a quick way to determine if some challenge or problem has arisen that makes it necessary to add the strategy to the agenda, subjecting it to a full discussion by the leadership team.

Returning to the example shown in the chart, the only item that belongs on the weekly or bimonthly staff meeting agenda is the one in red ("Highlight sacraments of healing within ministries"). The strategy "Identify & respond to pastoral needs in town" is moving according to plan (green), so there's no need at this time to take up valuable meeting time with it. The other strategy, "Attend to pastoral care needs of sacramental prep participants," has been delayed (yellow), meaning it has not progressed according to plan, but the plan has been modified and that change is communicated to the leadership team during the scoreboard review. Therefore no further discussion or intervention is required by the leadership team.

Other items compete for attention, of course, within any parish (like those shown on the bottom line of the scoreboard example). The scoreboard process acknowledges that while parish leadership is focused on top-tier issues, the parish staff is occupied with a diversity of still-important areas (e.g., worship and sacraments, faith formation, justice and service) that often require collaboration and problem solving by the full team. If one of these areas—all green or yellow on the above chart—were to turn to red, then it too would be placed on the meeting agenda for plenary discussion.

Through this system of prioritizing agenda items, you can save countless hours of time during the year by uncluttering and streamlining parish meetings. At times a discussion item will require more in-depth treatment, but it may not require the involvement of the entire team. In these cases, the agenda item should be moved to one of the two remaining types of meetings—ad hoc topical or quarterly/off-site review (explained below).

Summary and follow-through. About ten minutes before the close of the meeting, the discussion is halted and the designated scribe reads to the group the decisions that have been made and actions to be taken. This is not a formal accounting of every discussion at the meeting. Instead, it covers such essential information as (1) the agreed-upon actions by the group to move the strategies forward; (2) who in the parish needs to know about the decisions that have been made; (3) who from the meeting will communicate this information; and (4) the time frame for communicating this information to key constituents. This review process helps to clarify and gain consensus on these areas and how the group has determined to move forward.

Summary and follow-through help to ensure that the most important topics for the parish are being discussed and communicated in a timely manner. And while the example used here was keyed to a parish staff, this approach (with some simple modifications) could be just as effective for pastoral and finance councils, commissions, and ministry teams.

The Ad Hoc Topical Meeting

These two-to-four-hour meetings are limited to one or two topics that demand significant discussion. Because of their highly focused nature, ad hoc topical meetings give participants the chance to analyze and brainstorm crucial issues that impact the parish's long-term plans. They are specifically designed for key leaders and individuals responsible for or familiar with the topics under discussion. Advance preparation and research are usually required, and information should usually be sent ahead of the meeting so the session can be devoted to discussion.

My experience is that weighty church items are often mistakenly assigned to weekly or bimonthly staff meetings. The result is that matters warranting in-depth discussion receive insufficient time or, even worse, no time at these sessions. That sets up a situation where decisions are either rushed or not made at all, to the detriment of the entire parish.

The Quarterly/Off-Site Review

This type of carefully planned and highly structured meeting is generally meant for pastoral and finance councils, or for annual ministry leadership planning. The format—spread over one to two days—allows sufficient time and an off-site setting conducive to extensively reviewing progress on key issues, team development, goal-setting, and much more. It's important, however, not to overschedule or overburden these meetings.

If a ministry in your parish has an advisory committee, such as stewardship or worship, it should consider adopting the quarterly/off-site review format for its major get-togethers. Ministries like catechesis, which have more frequent work, might use a combination of weekly or bimonthly meetings and quarterly/off-site reviews.

Be aware, too, that facilitators can be a huge asset to your ad hoc topical or quarterly/off-site meetings. These individuals—from either inside or outside the church—typically come with a variety of skills and knowledge sets that can significantly improve the flow, content, and clarity of meetings. In the end, they can make a difference in terms of how much participants are able to retain and accomplish.

Endnotes

1. Adapted from Patrick Lencioni, *Death by Meeting: A Leadership Fable* (San Francisco: Jossey-Bass, 2004).

2. *Gaudium et Spes*, in Austin Flannery, ed., *Vatican Council II: Constitutions, Decrees, Declarations; The Basic Sixteen Documents* (Collegeville, MN: Liturgical Press, 2014).

3. "The preacher also needs to keep his ear to the people and to discover what it is that the faithful need to hear. A preacher has to contemplate the word, but he also has to contemplate his people" (Pope Francis, *Evangelii Gaudium*, The Joy of the Gospel [November 24, 2013], 154).

10

Managing the Liturgical Life of a Parish

Dennis Cheesebrow

For new pastors, few roles are more daunting than acting as a change agent for their parishes. Great expectations recede as reality sets in. They discover that change happens slowly, encountering resistance from many quarters. The failures tend to be remembered more than the successes, the pain more than the joy.

As a pastor you will know instinctively that change is needed. The good news is that through enlightened leadership on your part improvements can—and will—occur. The skills needed to effectively manage change across your parish can be learned, and the enabling tools and practices are known quantities. So, let's look at how you can put these resources to work to guide change from readiness to implementation.

The Pastor-Staff-Parishioner Collaboration

The mission of the Catholic Church is delivered through the dynamic relationship between parishioner, pastor, and staff/volunteer. Any new parish pastoral plan, initiative, or change in practices should be implemented through this collaborative relationship. A pastor can choose to assert his authority and bypass that union, of course, but it's usually ill-advised and unproductive.

The Importance of Mission-Delivery Relationships

Positive change is possible when relationships are strong and respectful; it's difficult, if not impossible, when they are weak, disrespectful, and insular. The change leader is the pastor, and by encouraging the development of mission-delivery relationships he creates an environment in which change can flourish. The mission-delivery point is the intersection of the three circles in the image above. When pastor, staff, and parishioners are clear about (1) the purpose or mission of the Catholic Church, (2) the vision of how it's carried out at the local parish, and (3) the shared outcomes, experiences, and goals that demonstrate everyone is on the same path to that vision, then they can better engage in a relationship of collaborative ministry and service.

Interestingly, as a parish moves toward meaningful improvements, voices of dissatisfaction will typically be raised. Parish leaders, for example, may balk at any changes in ministry that they've created over the years. Even diocesan-led changes may be viewed as unwanted or threatening. It's important to remember, however, that constructive criticism should not be discouraged but welcomed and respected and woven into the process of change. It should be a natural part of both change readiness and implementation.

Tools and Practices for Guiding Change

Data, Research, and Analysis

These are valuable tools that can help you to build a strong case for change within your parish, bolstered by the anticipated results. Data, research, and analysis provide an objective balance to human input, allowing the pastor and parish leaders to see the bigger picture and take a more systemic view of growth and change. Dioceses can often provide these information-based resources to pastors and parishes.

Enhanced Pastoral Plans and Vision Statements

Most parish pastoral plans that embrace change are plain, uninspiring narratives. They can be fortified through the use of numbers. For example, a parish vision of "high-quality liturgies that parishioners can't wait until the next Sunday to attend" becomes more powerful and meaningful with the inclusion of a measure: "The goal is to attract more than 60 percent of all parishioners to Sunday liturgy." Add a dash of hope and prayer, and pastoral plans can truly become energized and relevant.

Parishioners as "Consultants"

Parishioners need to be engaged at every step of the change process so they can see how their ideas and input are having an impact. The role and responsibilities of parish members in providing consultation and feedback on key decisions and parish planning need to be spelled out in written form and made accessible to everyone.

Transparency and Accountability

Be creative when it comes to communicating. One way is to post on the parish website and at every entrance to the church a quarterly statement of what is being accomplished by your staff, councils, and commissions, as well as what lies ahead. One parish celebrated its first anniversary of change by creating a wall of tissue boxes—eighteen feet long and four feet high. Each box was wrapped in gold paper and bore the name of a key accomplishment. Sometimes annual parish reports just aren't enough.

The Continuum of Change

Change readiness is the process of forming the key mission-delivery relationships throughout the parish. Change management is the process of implementing key points of change through those mission-delivery relationships. And those partnerships, in turn, drive the "4 Ps" of purpose, people, process, and performance that are integral to all change and improvement in parish life and ministry.

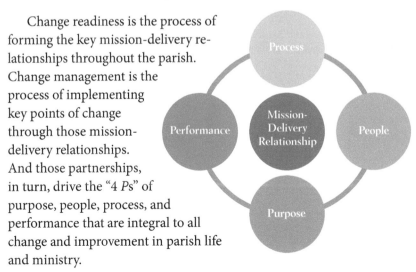

Change Readiness

During change readiness, the pastor along with lay leaders and staff use dialogue at the individual and group levels to establish a sense of shared identity across the parish. That communication helps to build and reinforce the belief that we can achieve what we set out to do—as long as we're in touch with the hopes and fears, the strengths and weaknesses of the parish and its ministries. Change readiness is supported by data, research, and analysis and by the other tools and practices previously cited. It also affords the parish a valuable opportunity to grow its social-networking infrastructure. This can be done by forming parish neighborhood groups or communities, for example, or through the use of surveys, focus groups, and listening sessions.

It should be noted that many parishes and pastors use pastoral-plan development or a capital campaign as the platform for change readiness. This is wrong since they are more appropriately acts of change management. Development of mission-delivery relationships and a shared identity should be considered parts of the change-readiness process (done prior to pastoral planning or a capital campaign).

An effective tool by which a pastor and key lay leaders can assess their preparedness to lead change readiness is described in the graph that follows. It has two dimensions: a fundamental appreciation of the culture of the ordained ("O") and an appreciation of the culture of the laity ("L"). Within this framework, optimal conditions for partnering and for the development of mission-delivery relationships exist at the center. High appreciations that skew toward the corners indicate conditions that are not conducive to partnerships and where leadership is hampered in its quest for change-readiness development and change-implementation management.

Very High

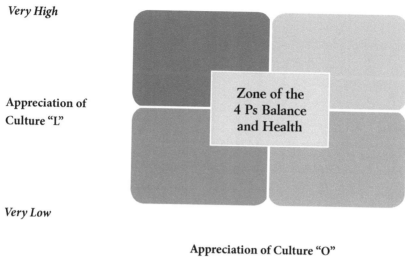

Appreciation of
Culture "L"

Zone of the
4 Ps Balance
and Health

Very Low

Appreciation of Culture "O"

Very Low   *Very High*

This framework has been used by pastors, finance councils, pastoral councils, and parish staffs to not only map out the current reality and relationships, but to track the journey of those relationships and challenges over time and across personnel changes in the parish, including pastors.

The example below describes an actual parish where the pastor operated in the lower left corner, the parish administrator in the lower right corner, and the faith formation director in the upper left corner. The result was an unhealthy, unproductive, and conflict-ridden environment where no change or improvements could occur.

To resolve these issues, the framework suggested that one to three people needed to leave or significantly change how they worked. Neither of those situations occurred. It wasn't until a new pastor was assigned to the parish who operated clearly in the center that two staff members left within six months. Consequently, parishioner registration, Mass attendance, and stewardship rose substantially within a year. And a new pastoral plan was developed, embraced, and implemented within two years.

Awareness to Action System Tool: Catholic Diocese, Parish and School Setting

Role of the Integrators of Pastor, Parish Directors, School Principal, Pastoral Council and Finance Council

The Free Agency Zone

High Appreciation of Laity Culture
Low Appreciation of Ordained Culture

Pastors, principals and directors do not effectively and efficiently manage their core processes, ministries, programs and services with growth of activities with little alignment to Catholic teaching

Individualism, confusion, with groups and people vying for power and privileges in the local parish and school

Experience of staff and parishioners of being left directionless, with little focus on mission, ministry, quality and performance

Catholic teaching with little substance or challenge

High levels of frustration with little focus on mission or ministry and little sense of communion

Growing financial instability and decreasing registered households, stewardship and / or enrollment

Low Appreciation of both Ordained and Laity Culture

The Leaderless and Lifeless Zone

The Political Zone

High Appreciation of both Ordained and Laity Culture

Open conflict and disagreement between councils, pastor, staff, and /or parishioners with local dissonance and noise a predictable and influencing factor

Self-interests overrun roles, responsibilities and relationships

Unity, performance and quality takes back seat to the "show"

Pastors and/or directors maximize "telling" and "controlling" and minimize excellence in staff and parishioner consultation

Departments and Catholic school operate in hard silos with little communication, collaboration or innovation

Resources are hoarded for local benefit, and truthfulness is lessened

Low Appreciation of Laity Culture
High Appreciation of Ordained Culture

Resentment and Passive Aggression Zone

Balance Zone

Pastors and parish leaders recognize the legitimate need for balance between the ordained and the lay authorities, roles, responsibilities, cultures, and gifts.

Differences are not treated as threats, and the local focus is the building of a vibrant Catholic parish and sacramental life, as well as Catholic education at the parish and /or local area

The key focus for shared ministry through distinct roles and responsibilities is the Mission of, and *in communio* with, the Catholic Church

Source: Team Works International

Change Management

As described above, change management is the process and act of implementing key points of change through mission-delivery relationships, and the shared parishioner identity and parish efficacy that develop. These relationships drive "the 4 *Ps*" of purpose, people, process, and performance that are essential to all change and improvement within the parish and its ministries.

In the graphic to the right, change readiness is reflected in the first two circles of "Individual Identity" and "Parish Identity and Efficacy," while change management is embraced by the next two circles of "Parish Pastoral Plan and Change" and "Individual Transformation."

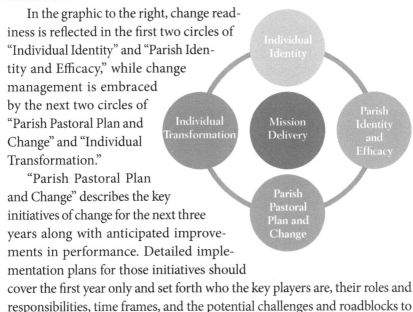

"Parish Pastoral Plan and Change" describes the key initiatives of change for the next three years along with anticipated improvements in performance. Detailed implementation plans for those initiatives should cover the first year only and set forth who the key players are, their roles and responsibilities, time frames, and the potential challenges and roadblocks to change. Ownership of action plans should be assigned by the pastor to staff members, councils, and committees, rather than the pastor taking on that burden himself.

Parishes and schools should integrate the key initiatives of a parish pastoral plan into a five-year (or longer) financial model that covers revenues, expenses (including staffing), investments, and fund balances. This long-range financial model should be reviewed and updated semiannually or quarterly.

Some parish leaders believe that they should budget and spend every incoming dollar of stewardship and gifts. A more effective strategy, however, is to budget no more than 98 percent of last year's realized stewardship, or no more than 95 percent of next year's anticipated stewardship.

Parish pastoral plans should be flexible and fluid and updated on an annual basis. They should also look out over a three-year horizon. It's advisable every fifth year to expand pastoral planning by staging a more inclusive event that features parish-wide meetings and communications aimed at involving everyone in the change process.

Individual Transformation

This final stage of change management involves stepping back from the large group focus of "Parish Pastoral Plan and Change" and "Parish Identity and Efficacy" to the individual level where change readiness began. Pastors need to recognize that pastoral plan implementation may be perceived by some staff members, parish leaders, and parishioners as a threat to their sense of being valued, being useful, or belonging to the parish, not unlike the grief that accompanies a personal loss. Indeed, transition and transformation are fundamentally personal (to test this assumption, try changing Mass times on the weekend).

Addressing these sensitivities requires creating opportunities for engagement and expression of ideas and feelings among individuals as part of a shared journey toward a deeper faith and more vibrant parish life. Focus groups, task forces, town halls, and neighborhood meetings, as well as parish-wide surveys, are examples of forums that can stimulate the dialogue leading to implementation of a viable parish pastoral plan. Keep in mind that a pastoral plan is fundamentally built on shared relationships grounded in the mission of the church, a shared identity as a parish community, and a strong collective determination that "we can achieve what we set out to accomplish." With that foundation, a parish pastoral plan can flow naturally from a robust change-management process to which everyone has contributed and feels an active part.

11

Parish Finance

Jim Lundholm-Eades

The parish finance council is just one part of a comprehensive system the Catholic Church has put in place to help the pastor and community discern the will of God for his people. The pastor, the pastoral council, the finance council, and, indeed, the whole parish community seek to do the will of God through the relationships they form. To that end, members of the parish finance council reflectively address parish financial matters and draw on their talents to offer competent and prayerfully considered counsel to the pastor about the fiscal affairs of the parish.

"Best practice" finance councils use consistent frames of reference to guide what they do, and a pragmatic set of tools to get the work done. The following three frameworks highlight the thinking behind their work.

Framework One: *Missio* and *Communio*

Parish finance councils create for members an experience of *communio* focused on *missio*. *Communio* is the experience of the Lord in the gathering of the faithful to do God's will. *Missio* is the great mandate given to the church by Jesus to carry his good news to the world. In Catholic tradition, articulated so well by Pope St. John Paul II, *communio* exists for *missio* and *missio* is always carried out in the context of *communio* (*Christifideles Laici* [1988]).

Why is this important to a finance council? Because a finance council needs to remain focused on *missio* as it executes its work as an integral part of the whole parish system. Whatever the agenda of the finance council at a particular time, *missio* must remain at the heart of the conversation about parish finances in order to keep its work from being about the parish as a "business," or about money as an end to itself. In short, *missio* puts the work of the finance council in perspective.[1]

Framework Two: Fundamental Relationships

Canon law holds that each parish *must* have a finance council (c. 537) but only *may* have a pastoral council (c. 536). Many bishops, however, make pastoral councils mandatory through either policy or decree (c. 536). The pastoral council helps the pastor choose pastoral priorities of the parish. Members prayerfully consider all the options in the light of what they know about the community and its needs and make recommendations on pastoral priorities and how to put them into action. Those items are often identified in practical terms as liturgical rhythm and practice, sacramental and catechetical programs, evangelization initiatives, pastoral outreach, and resources and preferences in staffing levels or positions. The finance council thereupon takes the work of the pastoral council and expresses it in terms of a responsible budget that meets guidelines set by the local bishop on diocesan policy, other guidelines that may be set by the pastor, and civil and canon law.

The key to the success of both pastoral and finance councils is the quality of the relationships between them, as well as with the pastor. This dialogue within the *communio* is one key means by which the will of God emerges and is made clear, and so the pastor adopts a stance of prayerful attentiveness to what these counselors are saying to him in their deliberations and recommendations.

Framework Three: Governance and Management

The work of a finance council falls much more into the governance frame than it does management, but it crosses both to varying degrees. The pastor, whom the finance council advises, governs the parish, and part of his responsibility is to ensure its proper financial management. Bottom line, it is the pastor, not the finance council, who is accountable for governing the finances of the parish and for daily financial management. However, the real value of the finance council lies in giving counsel to the pastor more in his governance role than in his management role. Governance here refers to giving the parish a "big picture" perspective in terms of direction (where are we going?), vision (how will we know when we've arrived?), action steps (how will we get there?), and perpetuity (stewardship of the gifts given by God to the parish and its people). Management refers to being organized and operating within the clear boundaries and direction set at the governance level in the parish. As a result, the council's core focus—expressed as agenda items—should be more geared to ensuring the perpetuity of the parish than to daily operational matters. Be aware that while the council may get involved in both, its central job is helping with the financial aspects of governance of the parish rather than fiscal operations. In most parishes, daily financial management resides with a staff hired for that purpose, an independent service contracted by the parish, or an office of the diocese set up to do management for parishes.

Pragmatic Tools for Finance Councils

Tool One: Targeted Information

Finance council members need to be informed about the financial health of the parish. Their deliberations are mission driven and data informed. For example, they use financial reports provided by the parish on a monthly basis to monitor how well the parish is meeting its ongoing fiscal obligations and aligning with the budget approved by the pastor. To that end, there are five questions the pastor and every finance council member should be able to answer after reviewing the financial reports:

1. What is the current cash balance in each parish account (checking, investments, diocesan deposit and loan fund, etc.)?
2. What are the principal balances for any parish capital or operating debt obligations?
3. Can the parish meet its current operating cash obligations during the next twelve months?
4. Can the parish meet its debt obligations during the next thirty-six months?

5. What unfunded obligations do not appear in the financial reports of the parish, such as deferred maintenance projects, legal settlements to which the parish may have to contribute, capital projects under discussion, or staffing increases being prioritized, considered, or at least under discussion?

Some parishes have a staff person prepare the answers to these questions each month in the form of what is known as a *dashboard report*. This is a summary of key information in a brief report (often a page or less) that goes to every finance council member before each meeting. Parish dashboard reports can become quite sophisticated, which is great if everyone is able to understand them. But if the report includes measures like financial ratios (e.g., common ratio, debt ratio), it may be necessary to help the pastor and other members interpret them.

Tool Two: Member Expertise and Competencies

Most finance councils consist of between seven and twelve parishioners who have expertise relevant to the group's work. Local diocesan guidelines often govern the composition and size of the finance council. For example, it is common for a bishop to promulgate a policy that finance councils consist primarily of adult parishioners who are active in the parish, while those who are not parishioners must be both Catholic and recommended by their own pastor. Some diocesan policies also state that finance council members need to have expertise in fiscal management, such as banking and finance, insurance, accounting, law, property management, and business administration. Some parishes even have a checklist of competencies they distribute to the parish when seeking finance council members to show the current range of expertise on the panel and identify gaps that need to be filled. The checklist is a great tool for other parish consultative groups to use when looking for new members to fill their ranks.

The pastor is always a member of the finance council. What's more, the council can only meet with his knowledge and approval since it's the relationship between him and the finance council (as well as with the pastoral council) that makes up the consultative system designed by the church.

Most policies and guidelines prescribe term limits for finance council members, often three years with the opportunity for a one-term renewal. If a finance council does not have term limits, the pastor usually establishes a staggered three-year schedule for term expirations so they don't all occur at the same time (see the *Catholic Standards for Excellence* published by the Leadership Roundtable at https://leadershiproundtable.org /drawer-catholic-standards-for-excellence).

Tool Three: Focused, Agenda-Driven Meetings

The work of the finance council has a predictable rhythm that enables the pastor and the chair of the finance council to establish an annual cycle of meeting agendas for the group. Indeed, an essential tool for staying focused is the meeting agenda. Every finance council meeting needs an agenda, and because of the predictability of the rhythm of its work, finance council agendas can be planned well in advance.

There are often two categories of agenda items: (1) those relating to the month-to-month monitoring of parish fiscal performance, and (2) those relating to the longer-term financial health of the parish. The matter of *when* these items are addressed depends in part on the timing of the pastoral council carrying out its duties of helping the pastor identify priorities and changes to programs, staffing levels, and more. Introducing any kind of capital works project or significant maintenance project also impacts the timing of the finance council agenda.

Ongoing monitoring of the financial health of the parish should be part of most finance council meetings. Agenda items might include:

- A comparison of actual revenue and expenses with budgeted revenue and expenses, and recommendations for adjustments to both in order to keep the parish on track with its budget. The budget report with the actual and budget numbers might also include percentage variance and dollar variance columns. Members of the finance council who have expertise can provide insight into whether these variances are significant.

- A review of the monthly cash flow (also known as "profit and loss") statement for both bottom-line performance and for any significant change or extraordinary expenses or revenues that might improve or otherwise change the financial position of the parish. Finance council members with professional experience in this area can provide insights and suggest key questions members need to discuss.

- Assurance that any taxes due for unrelated business income are paid on time to the IRS.

Agenda items that relate to the long-term financial health of the parish include:

- Evaluating the revenue side of parish fiscal performance against projections and making recommendations about revenue assumptions for the next two to three years.
- Reviewing revenues and expenses related to the new and emerging priorities and activities the pastoral council is considering recommending, and turning the findings of that review into budget assumptions for use if these proposals are adopted.
- Making recommendations for assumptions about revenue and expenses that will guide budgeting for the next fiscal year.
- Preparing a budget proposal for the pastor to consider approving that is based on the priorities the pastor has approved in consultation with the pastoral council.
- Recommending a responsible budget that meets all guidelines established by the bishop and the pastor. This is normally an annual budget, but many parishes are beginning to make biannual budgets, especially when capital debt is involved.
- Reviewing audit/review reports, especially any management letters, for deficiencies related to financial controls as well as to capacity to service debt.
- Standing by the pastor (sometimes literally) when he shares the final approved budget with the parish, or when difficult news about parish finances needs to be shared.
- Proposing a system by which all parishioners get financial information and have the opportunity to discuss it.
- Recommending updates to parish financial control policy and procedure as operating conditions, law, and diocesan policy change.
- Recommending staffing structure for the temporal administration of the parish.

On occasion there is a need for specific items to appear on the finance council agenda, such as:

- Examining the mission of the parish with the help of the pastoral council so that finance council members can identify the values and priorities that need to be expressed in the budget they are developing.

- Holding a spiritual retreat—including catechesis on discernment—so that finance council members can better participate in decisions and consultation in the context of Catholic teaching and tradition.

- Developing a fraud policy. According to a 2006 study by the Villanova University Center for the Study of Church Management, over 85 percent of dioceses reported financial fraud over a period of five years, underscoring the need to address this crucial area. A fraud policy is a standard protocol to follow—such as a mandatory call to police—when fraud (or theft) is uncovered. More than 93 percent of fraud cases uncovered in dioceses over those five years were in fact reported to the police and, of those cases, 91 percent were on a scale that made an insurance claim necessary.[2]

Tool Four: Investment in Time and Preparation

Any pastor inviting people to join a finance council should make his expectations explicit up front. They will invariably include the requirement that members do their "homework" before meetings so they arrive well prepared (e.g., having digested the current financial report). Finance council members are also expected to invest in developing a robust prayer life that includes asking guidance of the Holy Spirit, and participation in the liturgical life of the parish. Furthermore, they need to invest the time in getting to know other pastoral council members (meeting somebody for coffee is a great tactic) in order to understand their perspective on the parish's pastoral plan. Such encounters also enable finance council members to learn more about their own role in the parish. One of the best ways to broaden their horizons, of course, is to *read*. The documents listed in the resources section at the end of this chapter, which speak to the work of the parish finance council, are an excellent starting point.

Conclusion: Drawing Boundaries

Some matters are clearly outside the purview of the finance council. For example, the consultative forum for developing a pastoral plan for the parish is the responsibility of the pastoral council (the finance council applies its expertise to the pastoral plan). Nor should the finance council.

- do performance evaluations of staff members or make decisions about hiring or terminating employees;
- make financial decisions for the pastor;
- recommend policy or procedures that ignore diocesan policy, particular law established by the bishop, civil law, or canon law;
- sign contracts on behalf of the parish;
- make recommendations that are against Catholic teaching.

Notwithstanding these natural boundaries, the parish finance council enjoys a broad range of responsibilities that are integral to the pastoral plan and the mission of the church. Through their ongoing partnership with the pastor and pastoral council, the dedicated members of the finance council play a vital counseling role that ultimately leaves a bold mark on both the temporal and spiritual work of the parish.

Resources for Further Reading

A Sample of a Diocesan Guide for Parish Finance Councils

Diocese of Bismarck, "Parish Finance Council's Role and Responsibilities," http://bismarckdiocese.com/documents/Finance/ParishFinanceCouncils RolesandResponsibilities.pdf.

Easy Reading on Canon Law Related to Parish Finance Councils

Cathy Caridi, "Canon Law and Parish Councils," *Canon Law Made Easy*, https://canonlawmadeeasy.com/2014/10/02/canon-law-and-parish -councils/.

On Consultation in Catholic Parishes Specific to Parish Finance Councils

Brenda Hermann and James T. Gaston, *Build a Life-Giving Parish: The Gift of Counsel in the Modern World* (Liguori, MO: Liguori Publications, 2010).

On Communio *and* Missio *and the Role of the Laity*

John Paul II, *Christifideles Laici*, December 30, 1988, Libreria Editrice Vaticana, https://www.vatican.va/content/john-paul-ii/en/apost_exhortations /documents/hf_jp-ii_exh_30121988_christifideles-laici.html.

Standards for Finance Councils

Leadership Roundtable, *Catholic Standards for Excellence*, https://leadership roundtable.org/drawer/catholic-standards-for-excellence/.

Endnotes

1. See Brenda Hermann and James T. Gaston, *Build a Life-Giving Parish: The Gift of Counsel in the Modern World* (Liguori, MO: Liguori Publications, 2010).

2. See Charles E. Zech, *Best Practices in Parish Stewardship* (Huntington, IN: Our Sunday Visitor, 2008).

12

The Pastor and Canon Law

Barbara Anne Cusack

The Code of Canon Law will be fundamental to your role as pastor, helping to define your rights and obligations as well as providing an organizational structure without which it would be nearly impossible to govern. Like any body of law, canon law is also complex, and because people approach it from so many different angles, it's useful to begin this discussion with some basic context. We have church law and we have canon law. Church law is bigger than canon law. It consists of conciliar legislation, postconciliar legislation, liturgical law, particular law for a diocese or a country, proper law if you're a member of a religious institute, and custom, which over a period of time can take on the weight of law. What we'll be focusing on in this chapter is the Code of Canon Law for the Catholic Church.

The Code is basically a codification of law within one volume. General law is the universal law of the church; it's binding regardless of where you are territorially. Particular law is for either a specific group or a specific location. We have particular law in the United States through the USCCB, which establishes laws that are confirmed by the Vatican and are binding within the United States. We also have personal law, where religious, for example, have their own set of laws. And we have diocesan legislation.

Why do we even need law in the church if the church is about love? The answer is that the church and love are not in opposition. We have law to encourage, promote, and support life—the life of the individual and the life of the community, both now and in the future. Law is a servant of theology, just as theology is a servant of faith. If you think of theology as faith seeking understanding, think of law as theology seeking practice. Because law is subservient to theology, theology has to come first. You cannot read law outside of a theological context. If you do, you become very legalistic and don't understand the "whys" of what you're doing.

In areas where we have weak theology in the church, we may also have weak law. For example, Vatican II made an effort to begin talking differently about marriage, to talk about it in covenant language instead of contract language. The problem is, we haven't really succeeded in developing that theology. As a result, the law lags behind the theology. There's still a lot of contract language, which essentially works; it's not impeding anything. But not until the theology of marriage progresses and becomes more substantive in the life of the married couple—and that really means as covenant—will the law catch up.

The image I like to use for law, and the role of law in the church, is biblically based: the image of the church as the Body of Christ. Think about law—canon law—as the skeleton of the Body of Christ. It serves the same purposes as our own physical skeleton. It gives our body strength. It helps us move. We'd just be blobs on the floor if we didn't have our skeleton. It gives us support. And guess what? It's flexible.

The law has those same qualities. It exists to give support and structure to the church, to let individuals and bodies within the church move from one place to another. Think about it: if every time you sat down to deal with a case in the tribunal and had to think up a new procedure, you'd never get anywhere.

The Flexibility of Canon Law

How do we use law? Again, drawing on that image of the skeleton, the law is necessary but not sufficient for the life of the church. We may be divinely instituted, but we are also humanly limited, and if we didn't have some structure and some support we'd have a very hard time surviving as an institution. If all we had was the law, if the first thing people saw when they looked at the church was its law, then it would be as dead as a skeleton that hangs in a lab. It would not be a living, organic body.

The law itself is not sufficient for the church. It needs the flesh and blood and spirit to be the living church. As our physical bodies are flexible but become less so over time, so it is with the church's law. If I get a phone call from a pastor saying, "Here's my situation, what should I do?"

I rarely say, "Do this." Instead, I say, "You can do everything from here to here and still be within the limits of the law." That's where the flesh and blood of the living church comes into play. You need to look at the situation through the prism of your experience and your knowledge of the people involved and decide where you are going to apply the law. Think again of your physical skeleton and the fact some bones are stronger than others. There's a reason your skull is the hardest bone in the body. It's because it protects something very important. If I break my finger it may be painful and inconvenient, but it's not life threatening. But if I crack my skull, that's more serious. You need to look at law in the church in the same way. There are some laws that can't be bent, so you look at what's behind them. What value is the law protecting?

Let's consider the laws on sacraments. When the canons are dealing with matter and form of sacraments, they are quite firm. That's because they're protecting something very valuable to us, our sacramental life. But other parts of the law are quite flexible. I'm not suggesting that you break the law, but if you slip up and don't get a detail right with respect to another type of law, it might not be that serious. It won't affect the validity of anything.

To be adequate for the body, our skeleton needs to grow. To be adequate for the church, the law needs to grow. Canon law is not static. It evolves as a result of the experience of the church. We need a balance and a distinction between stability and rigidity. If our bones become too rigid, they break easily.

That's what happened with the 1917 Code of Canon Law. Keep in mind, we had no codified law in the church for a very long time, until 1917. We had, to be sure, lots of laws, but no codified law. Almost as soon as the Code was promulgated, however, the world and the church went through the most rapid period of change history had ever witnessed. And very quickly, the law was no longer adequate. We forget that on the same day in 1959 St. John XXIII announced the Second Vatican Council, he also announced a new canon law. But he wisely decided to wait until the council had finished its work before starting work on a codification of church law. Why? Because law needs to follow theology, and we needed to see what was going to emerge from the council to determine how the law should follow. And not surprisingly, since it was finally promulgated in 1983, the Code of Canon Law has changed multiple times. Pope Francis has been particularly active in promulgating changes in the law, none of which are related to any doctrinal issues.

Delineating Everyone's Rights and Obligations

We need canon law to be stable but not brittle. It gives structure to an organization. It stabilizes. It gives a human and organizational framework. If the law didn't tell you, as pastors, "Here is what is expected of you," people might have wildly divergent understandings of what your role is. And if you didn't have law to say, "This is what it is," you could be pulled—if you're not already—from pillar to post trying to figure out what you're supposed to do.

Not only does the law give you structure, but it also governs how individuals relate to a larger group. How, for example, the members of a parish deal with the parish at large. It's not like a shareholder-driven corporation where everybody gets a vote. Still, the law gives structure to a parish so it can function.

The law also prescribes how one group relates to other groups within the church. We want everyone, of course, to work toward the common good. But we have to be careful that one group doesn't interpret as the common good what is its own personal agenda. That can easily happen at the parish level. And if you don't have structure around how your organizations function, you can have a situation where, for example, the athletic association is dictating how the rest of the parish functions.

To reiterate, you will need to have structures in place at your parish that determine how one organization relates to another and how each organization relates to the parish as a whole. Canon law also exists to protect rights and to spell out obligations. We don't have rights in the church because they're in the Code of Canon Law. It's because rights are in the Code of Canon Law that we have the ability to defend them.

The 1983 Code went much further than ever before in delineating the rights and obligations of everyone in a church. There's a section on the rights and responsibilities of the clergy, for example, and another on the rights and responsibilities of the lay Christian faithful. Some rights are human rights codified within the Code of Canon Law. These include the right to one's good name and reputation. Because it's delineated in the Code, if someone within the church, within that organization, violates that right, I can make a claim. I can defend myself because the law has codified that right.

Some rights are ecclesial, that is, by virtue of your baptism you have the right to have the word of God preached to you. You have a right to the sacraments. And those are because of your baptism, not because it's in the Code. But if someone were to deny you a sacrament without cause, you'd have a hard time defending that right if it wasn't codified, if it wasn't written into the law.

Some rights are ecclesiastical by virtue of the office an individual holds. In your role as pastor, you will have certain rights and faculties that come with that office. They cannot be taken away at whim. A bishop cannot say, "I heard about that homily you preached last week. I'm taking away your preaching faculties." When you're a pastor, under canon law you have a right to preach. If the bishop doesn't want you preaching anymore, what can he do? He can remove you as pastor. And there's a process for that, as well, to ensure the church doesn't violate your rights.

It's really about balancing individual rights with the common good. The fact is I have a right, according to the Code of Canon Law, to make my needs and my personal opinions known to those in authority. There might be times when I choose not to exercise that right because I recognize it's not for the common good (for instance, if my speaking out, which is my right, might undermine the well-being of the larger group). My right didn't disappear. I'm just choosing not to exercise it.

I'd like to also point out that a set of principles was established to revise the Code of Canon Law. And one of those principles is that the law is to make clear the difference between external and internal forums. Law governs the external forum, that is, the external dimensions of life. There may be perfect consistency between what one should do morally and what one should do legally. But in the end, the law is going to deal with the legal and not the moral dimension. Be careful not to impose one on the other. Let me give you an example. In a marriage tribunal case, I must look at the grounds on which the validity of a marriage is being contested. That means putting aside my moral judgments about the life of one or the other parties. Only if that person's moral failings impacted the marriage within the scope of which the case is being tried are they relevant. I can't just say, "This is a very bad person and I'm therefore going to find the marriage invalid." I have to carefully weigh the legal grounds for doing that. I can't mix internal and external forums.

By the same token, you can look at any of the canons and ask, "What value are we trying to protect with this canon, and what action does it provide for us to do that?"

Affirming the Church as Community

With that as background, let's move to the impact of canon law on parish and pastor, starting with the definition of a parish we find in canon 515:

> A parish is a certain community of the Christian faithful stably consti-
> tuted in a particular church, whose pastoral care is entrusted to a pastor
> (*parochus*) as its proper pastor (*pastor*) [shepherd] under the authority
> of the diocesan bishop.[1]

Each phrase needs to be teased out a bit for a fuller understanding. Let's
start with "community of the Christian faithful." The original 1917 Code
of Canon Law defined a parish as a territorial region within a diocese
that had a church to which a pastor was assigned. So, it's a much more
institutional notion of parish than we know today. A modern-day parish, according to canon 515, is a "certain community of the Christian
faithful," so we flipped the definition around. That means we have to flip
everything else that goes with it. If the pastor is the one entrusted with
the parish, then everything he does is for the good of the community.
Under the 1917 Code, we thought of the parish as a benefice—a means of
financial support. No priest could be ordained without having a benefice,
a named source of income. In the United States we didn't have benefices.
So, the understanding was that your benefice was the good of the diocese
in which you were ordained.

According to canon 515, the parish is also "stably constituted." It is
thus presumed to continue its existence unless there's a reason for it to be
reconfigured. It's stable.

As for the phrase "in a particular church," we don't entertain a congregational understanding of *parish* in the Catholic Church. We are always part
of something larger than what we see before us. Indeed, the parish is larger
because of its connection to the diocese and its bishop. And through the
bishop, the parish and the diocese are larger because he is their connection
to the universal church. We really have to work against a congregational
understanding of the parish, especially in this country where we're so driven
by individualism. We have to work hard at making those connections.

As we're seeing, the difference between the 1917 institutional model and
the 1983 community model of the parish is more than just terminology.
It's conceptual and attitudinal. The 1917 Code cast the church as a perfect
society—an institution that maintains within itself everything it needs
to achieve its ends. Now, with the benefit of Vatican II, we talk about the
church as the *people of God*. We've shifted from perfect society to a much
more biblically based notion. Put another way, we've moved from institutional to communal.

Pastor as Parish Shepherd

As our next step toward better understanding canon law, let's change the focus from parish to pastor and begin by asking a fundamental question: What is a pastor?

Actually, that definition needs to embrace the notion of parish as a community of people. If you examine what canon law says about what your role as a pastor will be, the language makes little sense outside the notion of community. The pastor exists for the sake of the parish community; it's what gives meaning to the role and office of pastor. Pope Francis, in one of his talks, said a priest should smell like sheep.[2] He wasn't being literal, of course, but rather making the point that a priest should be so intertwined with his community that when someone looks at him, they don't see just him, they see his parish. It's the biblical notion of pastor as shepherd in the name of Christ. Pastoral service clearly takes precedence over the notion of benefice. So, when you take possession of your parish—and we still use that language in the Code—think of it less in terms of "It's become my property" than as "I've become its shepherd." You're putting your arms around the parish, not putting the parish in your back pocket.

In terms of your actual responsibilities, here's what canon 519 says:

> The pastor (*parochus*) [parish priest] is the proper pastor . . . of the parish entrusted to him, exercising the pastoral care of the community committed to him under the authority of the diocesan bishop in whose ministry of Christ he has been called to share, so that for that same community he carries out the functions of teaching, sanctifying, and governing, also with the cooperation of other presbyters or deacons and with the assistance of lay members of the Christian faithful, according to the norm of law.

An important takeaway from this canon is that as a pastor you are never alone in carrying out your responsibilities. Others within the church will be called on to share the pastoral role with you, including parish priests, deacons, laity, and religious. They assist you in fulfilling your responsibilities. The fact that you don't bear the full weight doesn't mean, of course, that you can simply relinquish all responsibility. In terms of *teaching*, you have a primary responsibility to see that the word of God is conveyed to all your parishioners, and that they are instructed in Christian doctrine. *Sanctifying* means presiding over the Eucharist, ensuring it's at the center of parish assembly and that the faithful participate in the liturgy and devoutly receive the sacraments.

Ruling, or *governing*, gets a little more complicated. The administrative responsibilities assigned by law to the pastor are many and varied. One of the most important is presiding over the parish pastoral council and parish finance council in order to receive the consultation necessary for the fulfillment of your pastoral role.

In other words, both councils will serve in advisory capacities to you. Sometimes people who sit on these councils feel diminished when you remind them they're an advisory—not a deliberative—body. True, you will be the ultimate decision maker, but decision-making must be thought of as a process that involves researching, evaluating the information, developing options, recommending a course of action, and implementing it. That's the continuum of decision-making—and the councils are involved in each step of the process. Suffice it to say if you use your pastoral and finance councils in that broad range of decision-making, they will invariably see there's great meaning to the notion of being an advisory body. You need to know what your diocesan norms are on these councils (they should be available to you), as well as what the finance council functions are in your diocese.

Another aspect of governing that will be entrusted to you is financial administration. When you are appointed pastor, you become the administrator of the parish. As background, the parish has a legal identity separable from its members and from the pastor. It's similar to a corporation, whose legal identity is independent of its stockholders, board, and CEO. In legal parlance, that identity is known as a juridic person. Juridic persons come into being in the church either *ipso jure*, by the law itself, or by a decree of competent authority. In the case of a parish, the law makes it a juridic person. As a juridic person, the parish has certain legal rights.

One of those legal rights is to acquire and use church property. How does the parish acquire property? There are multiple ways. The most common is through the freewill offerings of parishioners on Sunday morning. Other ways are solicited contributions—essentially fund-raising and special collections—and taxation, the assessment of which the bishop imposes on the juridic persons under his jurisdiction, including parishes. In other words, he has the right to tax in order to support the work of the diocese. However, it is not an unfettered right. He can only impose a tax that is moderate, proportional to income, and approved by the presbyteral council.

As a pastor you need to be knowledgeable about what property the parish possesses. Where are its assets held? Who is monitoring long-term investments? What are the property lines? What does the civil law say about cemeteries, and do those laws apply to your parish cemetery? You do not have to be an expert in real estate, investments, or law, but you will need to have the awareness required of a good steward of the parish property.

Your Administrative Responsibilities

Under canon law, you will have some very specific responsibilities as administrator of your parish. First, you must "exercise vigilance so that the goods entrusted to [your] care are in no way lost or damaged" (c. 1284 §2). This means you need to keep a close eye on your bank accounts or statements. You may well have someone in your parish in a part- or full-time bookkeeping role. But it will come as no surprise to you that some people, given the opportunity, will take financial advantage of the parish. So, you will need to be vigilant by knowing what's in those parish accounts. You should also exercise vigilance about property in your care by making sure you have the proper insurance coverage. You may think it's wonderful that you have an open-door policy where anybody can come in and use the parish facilities when they want. It *is* wonderful until somebody gets injured, and you get sued. You will need to be aware of who's allowed to use parish property, and when, under your current insurance coverage. And if outside groups are using your premises, you should make sure they have their own insurance coverage.

Second, you should make sure that the goods entrusted to your care are safe, even under civil law. So, if property is given to you as a trust, you need to preserve it as a trust. Be aware that civil law will respect your role as the trustee.

Third—and this is one of your most important responsibilities—you need to ensure that any stipulations of donors are honored and secured. For example, Mary may give $10,000 for scholarships at your school. This act of generosity puts the onus on you to keep accurate records. Don't trust it to memory. Too much can happen. You need to document the fact that Mary gave X dollars for scholarships to the parish school. And you need to know *how* she gave it. For example, did she stipulate that the principal of the fund was to remain stable and the income generated was to be used for scholarships? The best advice I can give is document, document, document.

Fourth, you need to keep accurate records of income and expenditures. This includes drawing up an account of your administration at the end of each year. You are also required to prepare budgets and annual financial reports by the norms of your diocese. Moreover, it is important to share the financial condition of the parish with your parishioners. The more candid you are with them, the more they will believe and support you when you seek their assistance.

Finally, be aware that while you, as pastor, are the administrator of the juridic person, you may not enter into any legal process, any litigation, without the permission of the diocesan bishop. It is your job to know what your legal limits are. Check your diocesan regulations for how to seek the bishop's permission if you are drawn into litigation.

There are two types of administration under your purview: ordinary and extraordinary. Ordinary administration includes everyday tasks like paying the bills and making payroll. Administration is extraordinary by virtue of the act (like putting a new roof on the parish school) or its cost. Be aware, however, that extraordinary administration can differ from one parish to the next. Paving the parking lot may be considered ordinary administration in one parish because it has the income to handle it comfortably. In a less affluent parish it may be considered extraordinary administration.

Don't make an educated guess at which category an expenditure or project in your parish falls into. You should check with your diocesan finance office on what acts are extraordinary—therefore requiring the permission of the bishop—and which are ordinary, usually meaning you can proceed on your own.

Canon Law as a Bridge, Not a Burden

I'd like to leave you with this thought: Don't think of canon law as a burden, or as something you pull off the shelf and throw at someone when you have a point to make, as in "it's expressly allowed" or "not allowed" under the Code of Canon Law. Rather, think of it as a bridge that gets you from one place to another. You'll find within canon law basic principles and a framework for fulfilling your responsibilities as pastor. But canon law does not provide an answer to every issue you're going to face. You should be looking for assistance—and wise counsel—from other collaborators, ordained and lay, including your staff and parish councils.

Finally, rely on the ever-present guidance of the Holy Spirit. I can't emphasize that enough. If you've got a big decision to make, don't go first to the Code of Canon Law. Go first to that place of silence and contemplation and ask for the guidance of the Holy Spirit. Then see if you can integrate canon law into your pastoral ministry in a way that helps you make good judgments on behalf of the community entrusted to your care.

Endnotes

1. *Code of Canon Law: Latin-English Edition, New English Translation* (Washington, DC: Canon Law Society of America, 1999).

2. See "Homily of Pope Francis," Chrism Mass, March 28, 2013, https://www.vatican.va/content/francesco/en/homilies/2013/documents/papa-francesco_20130328_messa-crismale.html.

13

Risk Management

John McGovern

As surely as the seasons change, we know we're going to encounter risks in life. That's why managing them in an effective and proactive way is so crucial to your role as parish leaders. No one can eliminate risks, but one can minimize them and keep them from spinning out of control.

Unfortunately, risk management forces us to step outside our comfort zone and think like lawyers, accountants, businessmen, insurance agents, contractors, and more. It forces us to wear a variety of hats and look at things differently than we otherwise would.

In discussing risk management, it's helpful to start with a number of guiding principles. First, good fences make for good neighbors. In other words, good rules, policies, and structures make for good employees and volunteers within the parish. When we develop rules that are concise, fair, and clearly understood, we get much better results out of our people. They become, in effect, good neighbors.

Second, an ounce of prevention is worth a pound of cure. We can do lots of little things now to prevent big problems later on. Put another way, we can manage risks before they turn into crises. Proactive steps such as financial controls, monitoring, audits, and inspections are far more preferable than lawsuits, bankruptcies, and devastating newspaper headlines.

Third, controlling risk will not make you friends. No one likes rules and regulations. Your employees and volunteers will look upon them as restrictive and unnecessary. But you still need to have them in place, and they need to be enforced.

Fourth, risk management is a form of stewardship. Because we're put in charge of great assets, we must relentlessly care for them. If we don't, we run the risk of squandering them.

Fifth, we need to be aware of "third parties." These could be outside people or creditors who can initiate lawsuits or visit other problems upon us if we're not vigilant. For example, if someone gets hurt on church property and doesn't have adequate insurance to cover their medical bills, the hospital may come after us. So, we need to think not only about the people directly involved but about others who add secondary layers of risk.

With that as background, I'd like to turn to three broad areas of risk management that will be particularly important to all of you as pastors and leaders of your parishes. They are legal, financial, and general risks.

Keeping Your Buildings Safe

A church's "physical plant" is the source of countless legal headaches. That's why I strongly recommend an annual inspection of your facilities. Physical plant inspections should include sidewalks, stairs, masonry, roofing, windows, and the like. There are many building inspectors who do consulting on the side who can help you with this. Or you may be able to take advantage of parishioners with special skill sets in the construction field.

It's smart to include funds for annual inspections of your physical plant in your operating budget. Somebody needs to routinely get up on the roof to ensure it's not leaking; somebody needs to inspect the windows to make sure they're working properly; and somebody needs to check the walkways and steps for loose bricks that could cause people to fall and break a limb.

Also be aware of your responsibilities with respect to any vendors you hire. Because of the potential for lawsuits, you need to insist that these vendors not compromise on safety—that they strictly follow Occupational Safety and Health Administration (OSHA) regulations and not leave dangerous electrical cords, for example, strewn across areas where people are working. You should have a current certificate of insurance on file before you hire any vendor. Remember, these certificates are only valid for one year, so requesting certificates annually from vendors is extremely important. It's not a bad idea, either, to have these certificates mailed directly to you from the contractor's insurance company to ensure they're not forged or doctored.

Being smart legally also means documenting all occurrences on church property. Someone might slip and fall, get up and say they're okay, and you think that's the end of the matter. That's a dangerous assumption. The reason is that individual has up to two years after the incident to initiate a lawsuit, and if they decide to do so and the incident wasn't fully documented, you could find yourself on very shaky legal ground. So, when any type of incident occurs on church property, it's best to document, document, document. That means getting a name and phone number, taking a picture of the site where the incident occurred, and getting the names and phone numbers of any witnesses. Just because someone walks away from a fall doesn't mean you should let your guard down. You need to be proactive at all times.

I'd also advise contacting your insurance company, even if there doesn't appear to be a serious injury. Someone trying to scam the system could suffer a back injury working in their garden, say, and try to pin the blame on a totally unrelated incident, like a fall at your church. Your insurance carrier might want to reach out and contact the party involved to make sure documentation is in place to head off any future wrongful claims.

Targeting Lawsuits by Employees

Let's turn to the employment arena, another fertile field for lawsuits. Those suits could be triggered by alleged age discrimination, gender discrimination, ethnic discrimination, or sexual harassment. Typically, they don't have clear black-and-white lines and are very difficult to manage.

Termination procedures often factor into employment-related lawsuits. So, if you're going to terminate someone's employment, you need to have a well-defined process based on solid documentation. That process needs to clearly spell out why the individual is being terminated, along with source documents to prove it, whether they be complaints or evidence of excessive absenteeism, tardiness, poor performance, and so on. Those documents need to be part of the employee's updated file.

It's always advisable to draft an "exit" letter when you terminate someone. It should state all the relevant facts, including the reason for termination and what documentation is available to substantiate it. Finally, the terminated employee should be required to sign the letter, and both of you should have a copy. This way, if a suit alleging discrimination on your part is filed six months or a year down the road, you have an accurate record of what the issues were and why you took the steps you took.

It's not a bad idea, by the way, for your parish to have an employee manual that describes in straightforward language the terms of employment: policies, expectations, vacations, sick leave, and so on. What's more, every employee should sign a letter stating they're aware of and have a copy of the manual. Such a document can be pivotal in the event a lawsuit is brought against your parish.

Among the key areas your employee manual should cover are policies governing sexual harassment. Clearly, your parish should have in place a zero-tolerance policy so that there's no question in anyone's mind what constitutes sexual harassment. It's particularly important that the pastor set the tone here, and if you see or are made aware of any behavior or practice that violates the sexual harassment policy, that you deal with it quickly and forcefully.

Mitigating Contractor Risks

Tax issues surrounding independent contractors is another high-risk area. When you hire someone and don't withhold taxes, you run the risk of improperly classifying them as an independent contractor instead of as an employee. A true independent contractor is someone who maintains a business with a physical location, phone number, clients, insurance and so forth; they may or may not be incorporated. If you have any doubts, take a look at the checklist the IRS has prepared to see if they qualify as a business or as an employee.

Be aware that if you hire someone as an independent contractor and the IRS says, "No, they don't meet the criteria," then the parish will be responsible for that worker's full tax burden, including income tax withholding and Social Security taxes at the federal level, and disability and unemployment at the state level. And those taxes are going to end up costing you an additional 30 percent of what you're actually paying that individual.

Worker's compensation is another major concern when hiring a contractor. As a general rule, independent contractors are not covered under the parish's worker's compensation policy; only employees are covered. So, let's say you retain an accountant and he falls down the front steps of the church and is injured. The parish's worker's compensation policy is not engaged; the accountant must use his own insurance. That's why whenever you hire an outside business, you should ask to see their certificate of insurance to make sure they're covered. Be particularly wary of undocumented workers and businesses. While your heart may be in the right place in giving the cleaning lady a job where you pay her without taking out taxes, you could be taking a huge legal risk if she is not independently insured as her own business.

Let me describe for you the magnitude of that risk. The state of New Jersey has a rule known as treble damages for worker's compensation claims. If the cleaning lady you've retained falls down the stairs at your parish, for example, and winds up at the hospital with no insurance, that hospital could end up spending $50,000 out of its own pocket to treat her. The hospital will be reimbursed from a special state fund created for cases like that, but in order to replenish the fund, the state will bill you, her employer, $150,000—treble damages, or three times the amount of the claim.

To reiterate, everyone who works at the parish must either be on the payroll system as an employee or have their own business with insurance coverage.

Financial Risk: Cash Management

Let's flip the page and look at our second major area of risk management: financial.

One of the ripest areas for trouble is the handling of cash, especially the proceeds from the Sunday collection. Specifically, you should have multiple teams of counters, and the same team should not count every week. Rotate the teams so that it's easier for you to spot any irregularities from one week to the next. In addition, all parishes should be using sealed and tamperproof bags for depositing collection proceeds, instead of the traditional canvas bags with the big zippers. Banks are on notice that if a seal is broken, they should not accept that deposit.

I also recommend that at least two of those counters sign the actual deposit slip. And here's the reason: if you're making a $5,000 deposit and have a signed slip to prove it, then this acts as a deterrent to a bookkeeper or anyone else from filling out and bringing to the bank an alternative slip for $4,000 and pocketing the difference.

Tight cash management should be employed for not only Sunday collections but school cafeteria money, bingo receipts, carnival receipts, and any other church event or activity where money is involved. Carnivals, in particular, can involve the handling of tens of thousands of dollars. So again, it's important to use sealed bags, teams of counters, and signed deposit slips.

You might think of cash as toxic waste. It requires extreme precautions in terms of how it's collected, where it's stored, who has access to it, and how it's transported. You also need to train your personnel in proper handling techniques. And to that end, you should have comprehensive procedures in place. It gets back to what I said above: good fences help to keep everyone honest.

Simple Ways to Detect Fraud

Speaking of procedures, one of the smartest you can adopt as pastor is to personally open every bank statement that comes in. In fact, no bank statement should be opened by anybody other than you. The reason is that you want to be able to take a close look at the bank's record of checks written by the parish to payees or vendors. In one recent scam involving a church, the names of legitimate, recognizable vendors were entered into its computerized financial books, but the actual checks were made out to individuals who fraudulently cashed them and kept the money, which eventually turned into a fraud of over $800,000. The scam was set up so that anyone looking at the electronic records only would never be able to detect it. The best way for you to combat this type of fraud is to scrutinize the checks and names of payees on the church's bank statement.

This practice should be applied, by the way, to every bank account you maintain, whether it's for the CYO, religious ed, home school, or any other. Experience shows that those small accounts can often be breeding grounds for fraud. Here's an example: You might go through your bank statement and see a check from the home school account written out to Costco for $2,000 for a high-definition TV. When you question the head of that program, she tells you yes, she wrote the check out to Costco but then paid it back with a personal check so that no one was cheated. She just wanted to avoid paying the sales tax on the TV. Well, at the very least what she did was defraud the state as well as misuse church resources. Again, a little vigilance on your part can help uncover these types of schemes.

Another good financial safeguard is to compare actual to budgeted expenditures. In other words, compare what's actually spent by a department against what it was budgeted for at the beginning of the budget cycle. If you have a maintenance-supply budget of $5,000, for example, and half-way through the year your janitor has already spent $10,000, it's time to ask some hard questions. I'm familiar with a case involving a maintenance man who was taking church supplies and selling them every weekend at a Pennsylvania flea market and pocketing the money. A budget comparison can be helpful in spotting this kind of abuse. What can really help you in this effort is commercially available software that makes the budgeted-to-actual expenditure comparison quick and simple.

It's not a bad idea, either, to have an accountant on your parish finance council. And be sure to ask that professional to conduct some random audits. Just knowing that someone is looking over their shoulder should help to keep everyone on their toes.

Being Proactive about Unpaid Tuition

The final area I want to mention under financial risk management is unpaid tuition within Catholic schools. This is becoming an increasingly serious problem as more and more parents are out of work and their discretionary money continues to shrink. The result is that tuition gets paid late, or not at all.

While as Catholics we're sympathetic to the plight of these families, we can't turn our backs on the financial implications it has for our schools. We must address the problem proactively by establishing a policy around tuition delinquency, and letting parents know upfront that if they fall X number of months behind on their payments, their children will no longer be able to attend school. Or you might specify that no child is allowed to graduate unless their tuition is paid in full. Your parish may have a "tuition angel" type of program in place to help needy families. But it's important to make sure these policies and programs are known in advance by everyone. It becomes a very difficult process to manage once a family has fallen two or three months behind on tuition payments and the unpaid amount becomes substantial.

Another sound piece of advice is this: if a delinquent family decides to make a lump-sum payment, require that it be in cash or a bank check. This way you prevent a situation whereby parents write a large tuition check, allowing their child to graduate, knowing full well that check is going to bounce. They've managed to abuse the system because you weren't more diligent.

Managing Contractors

Beyond legal and financial is an array of other risks you're likely to encounter as pastor. One of the biggest involves building renovation and construction projects. Because these projects can run into millions of dollars, I strongly suggest hiring what's known as a "master of the works." This is an individual with extensive construction experience whose job is to keep an eye on the general contractor and ensure that appropriate materials are being used and that no shortcuts or variations from original specs are occurring. Because the master of the works keeps the contractor on his toes and helps mitigate or prevent potential problems, he's well worth his fee. You might find a retired person or a parishioner with considerable construction knowledge and background who would be delighted to serve in this important risk-management role for the church.

When it comes to mitigating risk, sometimes it's better to just tear down a building. The Catholic Church has lots of old structures, and sometimes they're so antiquated and/or asbestos filled that there's no point in renovating them or even letting them stand. As the parish leader, you may need to make that determination as a way of cutting your risks.

Raffle games are another area that can get you in trouble if you're not alert. Make sure that any organization you team up with to run the contest is following all gaming laws and regulations, particularly as they relate to obtaining proper gambling licenses from the state and distributing raffle books across state lines. We had a case of a pastor running a super-raffle who apparently didn't know any better and mailed books all over the country, in clear violation of US postal laws. Also, make sure that you and any cosponsor are following federal tax laws, which require sending 1099 and W-2G tax forms to any raffle winner of more than $600, whether it's in the form of cash or a prize like a TV.

Keeping Computers and Information Safe

Let's talk a little bit about computer risks, particularly in the area of backups. I can personally cite the case of a business manager who was diligent in backing up all her files, only to become the victim of an overnight robbery at the rectory that not only resulted in the loss of her desktop computer but a box of backups that she kept nearby. The message is clear: all the backups in the world are worthless unless you secure them off-site. Robbery isn't the only risk: if a fire occurs in the rectory and the sprinkler system goes off, your backups could be destroyed. Still another example:

We had a bookkeeper who dutifully backed up everything but inadvertently left her portable flash backup drive in the computer at the close of work one day. When she returned the next morning, she discovered that a lightning strike had fried the computer and her backups, including the flash drive. So watch how your staff handles the backup of important information.

Three other computer areas you need to be aware of are firewalls, spam, and spyware. With respect to the first, you need to be sure that your tech people have built a firewall that's capable of preventing intrusions into your network and the loss of proprietary and personal information. It's important, too, that firewalls be tested on a regular basis by experienced companies to reduce the chance of a hacker breaking into your system.

Spam is also a serious problem because of what may be attached to it—software that captures and sends out proprietary data residing on your network. In a more mundane way, as most of us know, spam can clog your machines and make them work much slower.

By the same token, spyware can pose a severe threat. Once this software secretly penetrates your hard drive, it can collect bits of personal information and monitor your computing function. The way to combat this intrusion is through installing anti-spyware and anti-spam software. Remember that it, too, needs to be regularly tested and updated to remain effective.

Disaster Plans

Let us conclude our discussion on risk management by turning to disaster plans, which any parish with a school needs to have in place. Lockdown procedures are an important part of that plan. Lockdowns are emergency protocols designed to protect people from a dangerous event originating outside your facility, like an intruder trying to break in, or from the inside, like a chemical spill in the science lab. Lockdown procedures need to be practiced through periodic drills so that your principal and teachers have a firm grasp of when to shut the school down and when to keep students inside or send them outside the building. Remember to submit your disaster plans to the township and the chief of police.

The drills and precautionary measures you take may seem at times like an inconvenience or annoyance. But like the other forms of risk management we've touched on, they're a vital safeguard that protects you, the parish, and your people. Risk management really *is* a form of good stewardship and one that you and your staff need to take quite seriously.

14

Getting a Handle on Human Resources

Carol Fowler

The pastor of a parish has the fundamental responsibility to serve as a leader, preacher, teacher, presider, and person of God for his people. Under this umbrella comes the role of human resources administrator and, more specifically, being the leader of a diverse group of staff and volunteers in order to implement the mission of the church within the parish and link it to the larger mission of the diocese. That's why knowing some of the administrative practicalities of leading a staff will be so critical to your job as pastor.

Are you aware, for example, of the questions you're forbidden to ask during a job interview? Do you know what steps you need to take before firing someone, or why a cash arrangement with an employee is a bad idea all around? Or why performance reviews and job descriptions are two things you can't live without?

Human resources, or HR, takes in an incredible range of personnel issues, from recruiting and hiring to supervising and coaching to payroll and records keeping. While there's no way a single chapter could hope to adequately cover all of these, I'd like to draw your attention to a number of areas under the HR umbrella that you should have at least a fundamental knowledge of to be an effective administrator for your parish.

First, I'd like to dwell on four basic terms you need to know. The first two describe how we classify employees. The second two are on how we classify employers. For our purposes, there are two types of employees: exempt and nonexempt. Exempt from what, you might ask? The answer is overtime pay. There are two requirements for being defined as "exempt."

The first is the nature of the job description, the parameters of which are described in the Fair Labor Standards Act and subsequent rules from the US Department of Labor. The second is the minimum amount of pay that a person must receive to be considered exempt from overtime, even when the job description requirements are met.

It's helpful to know at this point what types of employees are exempt and nonexempt. Exempt are defined as those whose positions require a specialized course of study, usually through a four-year college degree. They include teachers, principals, site administrators, business managers, pastors, associate pastors, qualified professional lay ministers, and others having supervisory authority. As you may already know, what we sometimes do in the church is give a staff member a better title because we can't afford to give him or her a raise. For example, we may start calling the bookkeeper a business manager, even though this person still functions as bookkeeper. That doesn't necessarily mean he or she meets the requirement of being exempt. By the same token, if your parish secretary is still a secretary, it doesn't make him or her exempt if you start using the title administrative assistant.

It really has to do with the job description. And most administrative assistants, secretaries, bookkeepers, office clerks, librarians, and maintenance workers are classified as nonexempt. When employees are nonexempt, you have to keep track of their hours, requiring some kind of time-sheet records that are signed by both you and the employees and kept for three years. Most importantly, you need to pay nonexempt employees for every hour they work, and if they work more than forty hours in a single week, you must pay them time and a half. It's all spelled out in the Fair Labor Standards Act.

What you must remember is that one hundred percent of proof for an overtime claim filed by a disgruntled employee belongs to the employer, not the employee. And the only way you can provide that proof is to rigorously keep time sheets that are signed by both parties. You may assign responsibility for signing these time sheets to someone else with supervisory authority, such as your business manager.

Now for the two types of employers. The first is an "at-will" employer, defined as one who reserves the right under state laws to terminate any employee for any reason, with or without notice, with or without cause, providing such termination is not discriminatory. Most state governments give employers that right in their constitutions. And while at-will employers might seem to have a huge advantage, there's a bigger potential downside. It stems from the fact that if a lawsuit is brought against you as an employer, the defense attorney could use at-will employment as grounds for the client's case.

As employers in the church sector, we recognize that from time to time our legal advisors and advocates may use an at-will defense for a particular claim. However, as a pastor, you're always better off to think and act as a "just-cause" employer—the second type of employer—because it means you're more likely to do the right thing in a given situation. A just-cause employer is one who doesn't take corrective action, including termination, without having a clear, compelling, and justifiable reason. There are lots of just causes. You might run out of money, for example, and can't pay the employee. Or the individual may perform poorly or create a work environment so toxic that no one else can get work done. Regardless of the reason, we must always think of ourselves as just-cause employers and not take action against any employee without being able to unequivocally justify it.

Beware of Job Discrimination

As employers, we're also bound by the federal government's Equal Employment Opportunity Act of 1972. And that act forbids discrimination in a host of areas.

We may not discriminate, for example, against people over the age of forty. People under age forty are not protected by age discrimination. So if you decide you're going to hire someone who is over the age of forty as opposed to somebody who is under that age, you cannot be accused of age discrimination. Conversely, if you hire somebody under the age of forty versus somebody over that age and their qualifications are equal, the older candidate could file a suit against you alleging age discrimination.

As a longtime HR person, I can tell you that age discrimination is the thing we fear most. And that stems from the fact that hearing officers in age-discrimination cases will more often than not identify with the older people, perhaps betraying their own age bias. The onus is on you in the course of hiring someone to be able to show why that person is better suited for the job. You need to get specific about the skills or experience that makes him or her more attractive than the other candidate, and why he or she is a better fit for the culture and ecclesiology of your parish. And it can't be because of age.

Also, we cannot discriminate based on gender. The way this most commonly comes up is if we decide not to hire someone because she's twenty-seven years old, just married, and therefore likely within a year or two to have a baby and ask for maternity leave. In other words, we're not going to hire her because she may get pregnant. That's a classic example of gender discrimination. We don't discriminate against men because they're newly married and their wives may become pregnant, and we can't do it with women. For that reason, we're forbidden in the course of a job interview to ask a woman about not just age but also marital status.

Other areas where discrimination is forbidden under federal law are race, nationality, and ethnicity. Religious preference is one area, however, we are allowed to consider in the course of hiring. Under the Equal Employment Opportunity Act, we can—repeat, *can*—ask candidates if they're Catholic. We have that right as a religious organization. I would suggest, though, framing your discussion this way: "If you're going to come work for us—whether you're Catholic or not—you must live according to the teachings of the Catholic Church." In this way, we're telling people who are not Catholic that they still have to support our mission, or we can't serve as their employer.

If employees are required to live according to the teachings of the Catholic Church, then how do we respond to those who don't follow these expectations? My answer is to treat them the same way we would treat someone who's been drinking on the job. Our first response shouldn't be to fire them, but to help them deal with the problem. We might say, "We want to help you, and here's the name of someone at Catholic Charities (or another reputable support group) we think you should see." In the case of a person who is divorced and remarried without an annulment, we could say, "We'd like to help you do what's necessary to straighten out your marriage with the church." That, I think, is what our stance has to be: to make clear we want to support them because we deeply value their service and don't want to lose them as employees.

The Benefits of a Personnel Handbook

To give us guidance across the many sensitive areas of HR, it's important to have a set of just and clear personnel policies. These policies should be consistent with civil law. They should be fairly and consistently applied and communicated to all employees in your parish. And they should be compiled into a readily available handbook. Many times the diocese will send you a list of personnel policies and tell you to adopt them, giving you some leeway to make changes tailored to your parish. If a handbook isn't available, work through the diocese to develop one for your parish.

What kind of policies should this handbook cover? Major areas include pay scales, job descriptions, performance reviews, work schedules, and work-at-home policies. This last item deserves some elaboration. You might arrive as a new pastor and have three of your seven staff members tell you they work at home three days a week. If you're uncomfortable with that—and you might have good reason to be—you'd have grounds to say, "That's going to change immediately. You must be at your desk during regular work hours." And to support your case, you'd hopefully be able to refer them to the appropriate section of the diocesan/parish handbook on employment practices.

Other areas that might be covered under written policies include dress standards (business casual is appropriate for most parishes these days), children in the workplace (whether a parent can bring to work a sick child who can't go to school), and outside employment (it should be made clear that this employment will not infringe in any way on their full-time work with the parish).

On the subject of documentation, I can't stress enough the importance of maintaining a comprehensive file on each employee. As a new pastor you should carefully review each of those files soon after arriving. Find out, first of all, if they even exist and, if so, whether they contain job descriptions that make sense to you.

Job descriptions are a particularly effective personnel-management tool. They should detail the functions, duties, responsibilities, and reporting structure of each staff position. Why is this so important? Because the job description sets a baseline for your expectations of the employee. These expectations must be crystal clear to both you and the employee to prevent any ambiguities or misunderstandings. That's why I urge you to carefully review and then renew each description with the employee upon taking over as pastor. There may be times, for example, when the description does not reflect what you perceive the job's actual responsibilities to be. In these cases, you have the right to make changes—and make them quickly. Remember, a job description is not final until you as pastor say it is.

Be aware, too, that a job description should distinguish between *basic* functions and *essential* functions. Basic functions are, as the name suggests, tasks, duties, and responsibilities that support the goals and mission of that position. Essential functions are usually narrower in scope. They are those functions that, if an employee is no longer physically or mentally able to fulfill, might disqualify him or her from holding that job. For example, a maintenance person might be required to lift fifty-pound boxes of textbooks when they arrive at the beginning of the school year. If that employee becomes permanently disabled and can no longer perform that essential function, it could be a deal breaker. I suggest you go through each job description and put an asterisk next to each function that you deem to be essential, and make those designations clear to the employee. Failure to do so could result in your having to hire more help at additional cost to the parish.

No less important than job descriptions are performance reviews. These are written appraisals of an employee's performance prepared by the pastor and conveyed privately to the employee. This is your chance to tell a staff member, "Good job, but here are some areas I think we need to work on." Performance reviews should be, for the most part, positive experiences. And there shouldn't be any surprises for employees in these reviews. That's because if there's a problem, it should have been previously communicated to the worker. Employees need both positive and negative feedback—and it should be continuous. The purpose of the performance review is to formally capture and summarize that feedback.

The rationale is clear: if you don't tell people what the problem is, they can't fix it. It must be a two-way street. And if the feedback is negative, make sure it's communicated in private to the employee. You want his or her dignity and self-respect to remain intact.

Advice on Hiring and Interviewing

Hiring is one of the most important things you will do for your parish. As the saying goes in HR circles, "The more time you spend hiring, the less time you'll spend firing." Some other words of advice are "Don't settle." If you're in a bind to hire someone for a vacant job, don't compromise by hiring a candidate who is not fully qualified or totally satisfactory. You can always hire someone on a temporary basis, or a coordinator, until you find the right person. If that's proving to be a difficult task, you might have to review whether the salary is adequate or the job description is overwhelming for that position.

Interviewing, of course, is critical to the hiring process. It requires skills and ingenuity that may take you outside your comfort zone. You don't want to ask a question like, "Are you good at this?" and get back as a response, "No problem." As a good interviewer, you must know how to ask open-ended questions designed to draw the interviewee out and shed some light on his or her character.

There are actually two other categories of questions you should feel comfortable with. One is the behavioral question, which looks to the past. A behavioral question might be, "Describe for me a time when you had a really successful project, one where you worked with others and it produced a great outcome." You might follow up with, "What made it work?" "Who was on the team?" or "What was your role?" Another good follow-up question is, "Tell me about a time you worked on a project with a group of people and it didn't work out." Then ask, "What happened?" and, most importantly, "What did you learn from the experience?" I don't think there's ever a problem with somebody being on a project that failed. In fact, it worries me if somebody replies, "I was never part of anything that failed." That tells me he or she has never taken a risk or tried something different.

The second type of question that's used by skilled interviewers is the hypothetical question. It looks to the future and gives the job candidate a chance to solve a problem. For instance, you might say, "We've hired you as a director of religious education, but you immediately run into a group of parents so attached to the previous director of religious education that they won't give you a chance. They're critical of everything you do. How would you handle this challenge?" Hypothetical questions like this can reveal a lot about the person's leadership style, and you should be prepared with a list of such questions. Effective hypothetical questions often begin with, "Tell me about a time . . ." or "Think about a time . . ." or "Consider a situation in which . . ."

On the other side of the coin are the questions you must never ask during an interview. They include the age of the applicant, when he or she graduated from high school (since that would give away age), marital status or family plans, nationality, whether the applicant has ever been arrested, and if the applicant has any disabilities.

All these caveats, however, do not preclude you from checking with references on anyone you're thinking of hiring. In fact, it's absolutely critical that you check the applicant's credentials through others. And you're not restricted to the references listed. You can call anybody. You can ask anybody. If he or she has worked in other parishes, call the pastor. Find out why the applicant left. Just because the previous pastor says, "It didn't work," doesn't mean it won't work for you, however.

A further word of caution when considering a candidate's credentials: be wary of resumes, which tend to make claims that need to be checked out. Be skeptical if someone claims to have an MBA from Harvard, for example. Call Harvard and find out. People are forever staking claim to degrees and accomplishments that are exaggerations, if not outright lies. It's important to know this in advance, because how can you trust someone with the parish money or other valuable assets if you can't trust him or her to tell the truth?

Compensation Considerations

In the field of compensation, most dioceses have guidelines that cover their parishes. This can be very helpful to you from the standpoint of being able to tap into their information base. For instance, you might learn what the average salary of a parish secretary is in your deanery, and thus get a better handle on what you should be paying. Put another way, what would this person make if he or she didn't work for you?

One of the things you must take into account when making compensation decisions, of course, is the financial means of your parish. Since the buck stops with you as pastor, it's your responsibility to meet the payroll. Repeat—you must always be able to meet the payroll. You can't hand an employee a check on Friday and say, "Please don't cash it until Tuesday when the Sunday collection has cleared the bank." If you're having trouble meeting the payroll, you need to immediately seek help from the diocese.

A word on volunteers and compensation. The church does not pay volunteers—*period*. Even if you say to them, "I'm not really paying you, I'm just giving you a little five-dollar gift for every time you taught CCD," that could be construed by the government as dodging minimum wage requirements. If you want to give volunteers twenty-five-dollar gift cards at Christmas or recognize them with a dinner or plaques, that's fine. But be careful of anything else that has the appearance of compensation.

Nor should there be cash arrangements outside the payroll system for any full- or part-time employee. You sometimes hear of a parish cook or housekeeper being paid in cash. Why is that a bad practice? For one thing, cash payments make you liable for state and federal penalties for failing to withhold and submit income taxes on a quarterly basis. Secondly, it's bad for employees. Since cash payments do not count toward pension or Social Security benefits, they can leave employees destitute in their retirement years. The law is clear: no cash payments. All lay employees, as well as priests and religious, must be paid through the regular employee payroll. For religious staff (who have taken a vow of poverty), however, no taxes are withheld and no W-2 form is generated.

Centralized Benefits

Employee benefits are usually administered centrally by the diocese. And each diocese, by virtue of the contracts they negotiate, will have requirements governing access to those benefits: with health insurance, for example, those arrangements will specify how many hours a day or days a week an employee must work to qualify. As a parish priest, you can't change that. You have to abide by the diocesan rules governing benefits.

The diocese also sets the ground rules for most other benefits, including your parish's pension plan. It can be either the traditional defined benefit plan, or the increasingly popular defined contribution plans, like 401(k) or 403(b). Many dioceses have moved to defined contribution plans. Other centrally administered employee benefits include worker's compensation, family and medical leave, and unemployment compensation. Paid leave benefits include holidays and vacation, sick leave, personal time, family and medical leave, and jury duty.

And while it's not a benefit in the classic sense, I feel as a church we should allow our employees, particularly those in ministerial positions, time to attend an annual retreat. To be meaningful, it should be a formal-type retreat at an off-site location. You can even take money from your professional-development fund to pay for it. Look at it this way: it's important for you as head of your parish to foster the spiritual and professional development of your staff, and an annual retreat is a powerful vehicle for achieving that.

Finessing Terminations

Perhaps the most sensitive of your HR duties is terminating an employee relationship. It's useful to know that there are two types of resignations. One is a voluntary resignation, where an employee leaves of his or her own volition due to retirement, moving to another job, or a personal move to another city or state. Even though these terminations are usually on friendly terms, they still require thorough documentation. In short, you need the resignation in writing. A verbal resignation is valid and legal, but I would follow up with a registered letter that same day stating that you have accepted the person's resignation. That way it's legal and binding. And if no one else was present when the verbal resignation was delivered, I would immediately tell somebody—your business manager, associate pastor, somebody on your staff—so that you have a witness in case issues surface later on.

An exit interview should be conducted when employees resign. If they're leaving voluntarily, you'll normally have no problems getting their cooperation. It's helpful for you to ask questions like, "What worked well for you while you were here?" and the corollary, "What didn't work so well?" And you shouldn't miss the opportunity to ask, "What advice would you give me as pastor to make this a better parish?"

The second type of resignation is involuntary. While this scenario can often prove difficult for a pastor, it's not an unpastoral thing to terminate someone's employment. Sometimes it's the most pastoral thing you can do for the sake of the entire parish. The reason could be consistently poor employee performance, or perhaps the parish no longer has the budget for that position, or it's reorganizing.

Involuntary terminations can involve a host of issues—including severance, unemployment compensation, benefits, outplacement, and due process—so documentation is essential here, too. Another sage piece of advice is when you terminate someone, don't do it by yourself. Have your associate pastor or business manager with you, or someone from the diocese who has been through this before. Notice should be given humanely and quickly.

Some situations warrant immediate discharge. But most terminations for performance reasons should be preceded by warnings that spell out what the problem is, what changes are required, and the consequences if they don't occur. If the termination escalates into a legal matter, you may be required to confirm that you explained to the employee the nature of the problem on more than one occasion, and just as importantly, that you gave the individual adequate opportunities to correct or improve performance through coaching, classes, or other remedial programs. It's important that *you* feel good that you did everything you could to avoid firing the employee. Which brings us back to the importance of performance reviews, as discussed earlier.

Any time you have a situation that looks like it could result in a discharge, it may be helpful to get your diocese involved. They typically have a human resources professional who can assist you in achieving an outcome that is fair to both the employee and the church, and that can be defended if legally challenged.

A Helping Hand

What I've given you in this chapter is merely an entrée to the kinds of HR issues and responsibilities you must grapple with as administrative head of your parish. While the tasks may seem daunting, you can take some comfort in drawing upon an established network of professionals for guidance and support. Aside from your diocese, there's the Leadership Roundtable. This nonprofit organization of business leaders is committed to helping pastors and parishes adopt best practices not just in the field of HR but also in fiscal management, governance, and fund-raising. Another resource is the Villanova Center for Church Management, which offers a variety of learning programs for new pastors. And the National Association of Church Personnel Administration (NACPA) is a good resource to know about.

Time Management and Balancing Roles

Jim Dubik

We have all the time there is. So the real question is whether we use all the time we have well, or poorly. But even that question doesn't quite get to the heart of the matter. When you come right down to it, time is a metaphor for energy and focus. When we ask ourselves whether we're using our time well, the question we're really asking—or should be asking—is this: Am I focusing my energy on the important or trivial? Time is just the way we measure where we place our focus and energy. In this chapter I hope to present a way to first think through what is important relative to your role as pastor, and then translate the result of that thinking into a way to increase the probability of focusing on the important. No methodology is perfect; we shouldn't expect that, especially those of us who lead people in human organizations. But a disciplined approach to managing time should increase the time you spend on what is truly important.

I've been lucky in my life. I've had over 37 years of experience as an army officer leading mission-driven organizations, some as small as 20 people and others as large as 46,000; some were all-American organizations and others were made up of multiple nationalities and religions; sometimes my unit was located in one geographic place and other times it was dispersed over dozens of locations; sometimes I led in war and other times at peace. But I've not had a job. My life has been a life of service to something larger than myself, and I've led people who wanted to connect their lives to something greater than themselves, too. As I reflect on my life, I was never overly busy when I was involved in something important.

Rather, I was excited and so were those I led, for our lives had meaning. I imagine it's been the same for you!

Throughout much of my career, I've employed the time-management program that I advocate in this chapter. I didn't need a "system" when I was leading small organizations, but that didn't last long. As soon as I started working on the staff of a large organization, I realized that I needed a way to make sure I was focused on the right stuff. And when I started to command, even as a deputy commander, that need smacked me in the face. Some of the approach I will describe I learned in the school of hard knocks. But some I learned through the advice and example of seniors, peers, and juniors as well as through reading and experimenting.[1]

The processes that I use in this chapter are drawn from my military experience. Each of you reading will have to evaluate what I suggest to determine how to adapt the methodology to fit your particular situation as pastors, just as I had to adapt what worked in the corporate world to fit my military world. My intuition is that much of what I write will be useful to you, but some of it may not be. None of us can simply take what works in one context and apply it blindly to another. But we can learn from one another and modify best practices from one context to fit another.

Before I begin, however, I think a few words about leadership and management are in order. From my perspective the two are related, but different. You lead people and manage things. Leadership is about relating people to each other and to a common purpose. Leadership is essentially a "ministry of presence." You have to know and be with people to lead them. You have to share in their lives, participate in their celebrations and sorrows. Paratroopers have a saying: "It's hard to be uppity when you're jumping from the same plane, hitting the same ground, and living in the same hole." Leaders create followers by their presence and their example. Leaders create followers by providing vision, direction, and motivation. "Follow me" is the motto of the US infantry, not "Go that way; I'll be with you in a minute."

Management is about efficiency. You manage things, processes, and resources. Management is about organizing ways of doing things into transparent, repeatable processes so that the organization runs smoothly. Management affects mission as much as leadership. Soldiers don't follow commanders, even if they're great leaders, whose units run poorly. For example, when transportation doesn't arrive on time, mail is always late, promotions arrive but the corresponding pay does not, equipment doesn't work because maintenance isn't done on schedule, or food and resupply show up late or go to the wrong place altogether, soldiers don't conclude that they have a great leader; they conclude that they're in a screwed-up unit. Furthermore, they realize that they can't accomplish their mission under this kind of poor management. Followers are pretty savvy people. They link three things together, correctly so in my view: mission, leadership, and management.

So creating a time-management approach is a matter of freeing up time to lead, preserving and regenerating the energy to lead, and ensuring the management of the organization is efficient. Now, we're ready to start.

Thinking

We have only one life, and it's a multidimensional life. Simultaneously we could be a son or a daughter, a brother or a sister, an aunt or an uncle, and a leader and a follower. Each of our lives has a spiritual dimension as well as physical, intellectual, and moral dimensions. We each live in a complex set of contexts: family, social, political, and religious, to name just a few. Figuring out what's important, therefore, is a lot harder than it seems on the surface; each of us has to answer some hard questions. And even after we answer them, things will change. That's because life never stands still. You can't put your life on pause, so to speak, while you're leading an organization. So any methodological approach to managing time has to fit the reality in which we live and lead.

Step One: Identify Your Big Rocks

The first challenge you face is how to "fill the jar" of your life. In *First Things First*, Stephen Covey asks us to imagine the challenge of getting big rocks, little rocks, and sand into a container.[2] If you fill the jar with sand and the little rocks first, you won't get the big rocks in.

The question is: What are your big rocks? Big rocks come in two categories: personal and organizational.

Your personal big rocks first have to do with what you need to preserve and regenerate leadership energy, and second with maintaining key relationships in your life. I knew, for example, that when I deployed to Baghdad in 2007 and 2008, leadership in that environment would take a heavy emotional toll, and every day I would have to start afresh. To do that,

I'd have to be at my best, which meant that I'd have to get proper rest (and for me that's six to eight hours a night), have a vigorous workout schedule (one to two hours a day), time for prayer (one hour a day), and time for writing letters necessary to maintain my relationships with my wife, children, brothers and sisters, dad, and friends (another hour a day). The total time for personal big rocks came to ten to twelve hours a day. I reduced this by one hour by using as prayer time the time in flight or transit from Baghdad to one of the many activities for which my unit was responsible. That left thirteen to fifteen hours a day for "work." That time was filled with my organizational big rocks.

Step Two: Discover Your Organizational Big Rocks and Perennials

You're going to need some help with discovering "organizational big rocks" and what might be called "perennials." Organizational big rocks come in two varieties: leading and managing.

To discover your leadership big rocks, you'll have to analyze your parish and ask some questions. You start with getting an understanding of where your parish is—what it does well and what it does not so well, what part of its mission is strong and what part might be weak, where it is healthy and where it is sick, and where your people are thriving and where they may be floundering. Starting here will help you identify where your parish is and where it ought to go. Leadership takes place in the space between "is" and "ought."

Once you know where your parish is strongest, you'll have to allocate enough time to maintain that strength. Don't assume maintaining strength can be put on autopilot. You will not have to allocate a lot of time to maintenance, but you'll have to allocate some. You'll want to visit these activities enough to keep them going strong. So list these strengths and figure out how often you have to visit them to keep them on track: Daily? Weekly? Monthly? Quarterly? Semiannually? You can figure this out by talking to both the leaders and participants of each activity.

Then analyze your parish's areas of weakness. This may take a bit of time, too. To get an adequate understanding of what is really wrong, you will probably have to have a set of discussions with leaders in the various parts of your parish as well as those who may work with them. Once you have a good sense, you will then be able to determine how often you have to visit with parish leaders to do your part in improving whatever is awry. Once things seem back on track, you'll be able to reassess your frequency allocation.

You will have some "management big rocks," too. Every organization has them. Personnel, finance, facilities and equipment maintenance, training, ministry planning, and supplies and logistics are all examples. You should try to make a complete list of the management expectations that your parish has of you. As with your "leadership big rocks," you will have to map these out with regard to frequency. Which of these management responsibilities are weekly, monthly, quarterly, semiannual, or annual? In some cases, you will find that they are ad hoc—that is, they don't happen on a routine schedule. (Note: You should change "ad hoc" to "preplanned." Your parish will run more smoothly.)

Finally, identify your recurring responsibilities—your "perennials." Every leadership position has these. Some will be representative. For example, in one of my commands, every February I had to hand out awards at the annual volunteer recognition dinner, every March I had to represent the armed services in a local city's parade, every July I was expected to open the Fourth of July celebration, and every December I had to participate in a tree-lighting ceremony. Other responsibilities will be meetings or conferences that your bishop may expect you to attend—monthly, quarterly, semiannually, or annually. Still others might be reports that only you can write.

If you're lucky, you can look at your predecessor's calendar and find these events. If you're not so lucky, then you may have to ask someone to help you do the investigative work to create this list. Lucky or not, identifying these kinds of responsibilities early prevents surprises later on.

Without doubt, once you've discovered your big rocks and perennials, you will be like I have been many times—realizing that I can't possibly meet all these demands. Be not afraid: you have reached the assessing and divesting phase of step two.

Put all your big rocks and perennials on a calendar, or do a matrix, or whatever display with which you are comfortable. A visual representation is important at this phase because now you will have to determine which, among the many things you seem to have to do—or that others are expecting you to do—are those that you really must do. On your visual, mark those you must do and those that only you can do. The rest are opportunities to divest or to delegate—in the words of a former boss of mine, "Opportunities to allow others to shine."

Do this analysis with the help of a set of trusted leaders in your parish. I would often do this assessment with my deputy, my senior enlisted advisor, and my subordinate commanders—five to eight people. I have always found wisdom emerged from such collaboration. When a group saw the full nature of the challenge, each member felt a need to help identify solutions. In a parish, especially one where a pastor may not even have an assistant, the group should include one or two members of the staff and another two or three lay leaders.

You will want to set up a "we're in this together" dynamic in the group looking at your visual. If you are able to do that, members will start thinking out loud. You want to get to the point in the discussion where they begin to suggest that some of what you have identified as things only you can do are things one of them can actually do. And you want to get the discussion to the point where members look at the things you have on the visual but not identified as "your tasks" and say either, "That's not a reasonable expectation, let's do that another way," or, "You can't possibly do that, let's ask so-and-so to take that on." In this way, you can begin divesting those responsibilities and expectations to others in the parish.

Doing so frees time for you to lead and focus only on the important management tasks. Delegating also develops leadership capacity throughout your parish and creates cohesion among your parish leadership team. Delegating always surprised me. In these discussions, some people who stepped up to take on a task were those I didn't expect would—because they were either, mistakenly in my mind, too inexperienced, unwilling, or already too busy. If no one steps up, either you've identified something that your parish really doesn't have to do, or you've found a necessary activity in need of a leader. Finally, once you've finished delegating, set up a monthly meeting for those who have accepted new responsibilities so that they have a forum to keep you informed of their actions and where they can ask for more guidance if they need it.

We're now ready for the last step in the thinking phase.

Step Three: Allocate Percentages, Get a Sanity Check, and Adjust

Now it's time to ask yourself, how much energy must I spend on leading and managing? The answer to this question will come in a time percentage.

Remember, the time you need to regenerate comes "off the top." By way of example, let's use eleven hours as regeneration time and thirteen hours as leadership and management time. This means that 46 percent of each day is allocated to regenerating your leadership energy. It also means that 54 percent of the time, you will be fully energized for your parish—that's

54 percent that will go toward the leadership tasks that you've identified and to your management tasks and perennials, as well.

You should end up with a leadership and management task list and an appropriate time allocation, one that fits the needs of your parish as you and your team determine it.

Executing

In most organizations, the secretary or administrative assistant has the responsibility to prepare the leader's schedule. In some larger organizations, that responsibility may be shared among a chief of staff, a personal assistant, and an executive assistant. In some smaller organizations, like a parish, the pastoral leader may make his own schedule. In what follows, I address those situations where the pastor is creating his own schedule.

Set Some Boundaries and Rules

Creating your schedule needs some ground rules. Here are some examples:

- All meetings have an agenda, a person in charge, and start and end times.
- Meetings will run no more than two hours, with fifty-minute meetings being optimal, unless approved beforehand.
- Travel time between meetings and events is part of the schedule.
- Allocate at least fifteen minutes between meetings, if no travel time is involved.
- Start the daily schedule at 9:00 a.m. (unless you've got an earlier Mass!), and don't schedule anything after 6:00 p.m., unless it's an approved official function (like a parish council meeting!).
- Schedule no more than three evening functions per week.
- Schedule no official public functions on your day off.
- Stop the official schedule at 3:30 p.m. the day before your day off.

Your rules will be different. They will reflect your personality and style as well as the needs of your parish and the demands your mission places upon you.

I also limited advance distribution of my calendars. Only key members of my staff had access before the schedules were locked in. Early in my leadership development, I opened access to all. That was a mistake. What I found was that subordinate leaders, staff, and even community leaders would look for "white space" (that is, time on the schedule with nothing on it) and attempt to fill it up. As a leader, I wanted to preserve "white space" for thinking or spontaneity—or prayer! Ultimately, I learned how to limit access so that the right set of people could collaborate in creating my schedule and calendar but not so many that the scheduling lost its discipline.

Rules like these create boundaries for your parish staff. Without them, a pastor's life can easily become a solely professional or public affair. Or life can become so harried that it is unlivable. Rules like these are also necessary to preserve a pastor's regenerative time. And they're necessary as a "prioritization-forcing function." A leader normally has more to do than time to do it. Putting boundaries in place forces you (and your parish staff) to prioritize and divest constantly. Of course, there are exceptions to every rule at times, but that's what they are: exceptions, not the rule.

Create a Schedule, Follow It, and Note Changes

With the rules and time allocations in place and your big rocks and perennials identified, you can get to work on creating your schedule, and then following it. This step may seem self-evident, but it is not. Following the schedule is important for several reasons. It demonstrates a level of organizational integrity—that is, the organization and the leaders within it do what they say they're going to do. Following the schedule also produces predictability within your parish and creates the space for your staff to use their initiative. When a staff member knows that he or she will see the pastor on a predictable schedule, that staff member is less tempted to conduct a "hallway ambush" or have a "drive-by" office call.

Predictability helps you, as well. You'll know that the "big rocks and perennials" methodology ensures a visit to every key aspect of the parish organization and every staff member at a prescribed frequency. Emergencies always happen, and every leader should stay open to them. But, absent emergencies, following a schedule based on a well-thought-out methodology can be a stabilizing force within your parish.

At the end of the day, review how the actual day compared to the schedule. Doing so will provide the grist for the next aspect of the time-management methodology: assessing and adapting.

One final word: When creating your own schedule, as I do now in retirement, the actions above are still necessary. In fact, they may be more necessary because acting alone provides less oversight and increases the chances of poor use of a leader's time.

Assessing and Adapting

Once a month, a good pastoral leader should review how he actually spent time relative to the time-allocation goals set. The purpose is not just a factual review, but an opportunity to analyze why execution differed from goals and then to adjust goals, if necessary. The review should also include a task/frequency matrix. The matrix provides the leader another view as to whether he or she is focused on the important things.

If the difference between actual and planned time is small, you can usually ignore the difference. But in those cases where the difference is large, the pastor must dive deeper to understand why the difference emerged. Further, month-to-month differences also require investigation. Sometimes the differences are explained by an unusual set of circumstances or requirements, so no adjustments are needed. Other times, the disparity lacks an adequate explanation, so reinforcing methodological discipline may be in order. When a disparity persists, however, the pastor must question the allocation of time, figure out a way to divest some of the tasks in that category, or identify other corrective actions. But all these decisions are data based; further, the data results from the goals set because of a thorough leadership and management analysis.

Absent a time-management system like the one described, a leader usually has no idea how he or she is spending time or focusing energy—the pastoral leader's most important resources.

Conclusion

At first blush you may think that using a system like this is too much. I ask you to think again. Most of the work necessary to use this kind of methodology is "up-front" leadership work: the kind of organizational analysis any good leader does when he or she comes to a new organization, or the kind good leaders do periodically to ensure their organization is doing what it should be doing and operating as efficiently as possible. Further, it's the kind of analysis that a good leader does to ensure the organization's mission and its staff are fully supported and free of obstacles the organization itself creates to inhibit accomplishing its mission.

I've seen some really creative uses of a leader's time. Some, for example, use meals as "leadership time." One commander held weekly breakfasts at his house, rotating different groups of leaders each week; another used weekly lunches at various dining facilities throughout his command for the same reasons but with different sets of leaders. I've also seen some leaders use their exercise time to invite selected members of their command, some leaders and others not, to run with them. One way to look at "tricks" like these is from the perspective of maximizing the use of time. Another way is from the perspective of preserving regenerative time.

However leaders approach their time, time management remains a surrogate for the ways in which leaders focus their energy and attention on the important. We have all the time there is, and if leaders use it well, most often it's enough. I guess it *has* to be, because we're not getting any more.

Endnotes

1. Three of the books I use on a recurring basis are these: Stephen R. Covey, A. Roger Merrill, and Rebecca R. Merrill, *First Things First* (New York: Free Press, 1994); Jim Loehr and Tony Schwartz, *The Power of Full Engagement* (New York: Free Press, 2003); and Stephen Rechtschaffen, *Time Shifting: Creating More Time to Enjoy Your Life* (New York: Doubleday, 1996).

2. See Covey, Merrill, and Merrill, *First Things First*, 88ff.

16

Wellness

Andrew F. Kelly

At a convention on training for the priesthood, Pope Francis observed that young men who are psychologically unstable without knowing it often seek strong structures to support them, such as the police or the army, but for some it is the clergy: "When I realize that a young man is too rigid, too fundamentalist, I do not have confidence [about him]; in the background there is something that he himself does not know. . . . [Keep your] eyes open to the mission in seminaries."[1]

For the past twenty-five years, as director of the Clergy Consultation and Treatment Service at St. Vincent's Hospital in Westchester, New York, I've had the honor of working with hundreds of priests who have welcomed me into their interior lives. My goal in this chapter is to share with you some of that knowledge and experience in the hope you may avoid in your priesthood the kind of problems I've observed in others. It's also my fervent hope you will learn the skills of awareness, healthy coping, and self-care that can lead to a happy and fulfilling life as a pastor.

Because the priesthood is more a way of life than just a job, it's useful to our discussion to pose this question at the outset: *Whose priesthood is it?* You need to be clear on this. You're not doing it for mom, dad, or someone else. You're not doing it for the external reward of prestige, or because you need a ready-made role or identity. And you're not doing it to work out internal conflicts, which are best solved through the adoption of a code of conduct.

We start with this question because you cannot build a solid internal structure on external needs. To be sure, your priesthood will collapse without a strong internal foundation. For that reason, there can be only one answer to the question, Whose priesthood is it? *It has to be yours.*

Separating from the Laity

One approach to the theory of role identity sees a strong distinction between priests and laypeople. It holds that some people enter the priesthood to adopt a ready-made identity, to overcome a core of shame, and may use ordination as a way to bolster self-esteem and set themselves apart from others. In this version, negative qualities that could be associated with the laity (lust, substance abuse, depression, neediness, and being victimized as a child) are minimized by adoption of the in-group identity of clergy. The danger here is a failure to recognize the real self, as in "I am not one of them—I am a priest." Equally troublesome is its corollary, "I do not really need to be concerned with *me*. That is selfish. I care for others."

What this disconnection ignores is the fact that you are a human being entrusted with the care of yourself. You have the same human needs, the same temptations and risks as the laity. To attempt to compensate for this by adopting an identity is not to deal with one's issues—it's to bury, camouflage, and deny them. It's to deny internal awareness. Also implicit in this approach is an effort to diminish the laity and elevate oneself, which runs counter to what the church teaches in the *Program of Priestly Formation*. It holds, "A man of communion [is] a person who has real and deep relational capacities, someone who can enter into genuine dialogue and friendship, a person of true empathy who can understand and know other persons" (183c).[2] How does one accomplish this by setting oneself apart?

Caring for yourself is essential. Having self-knowledge and accepting your humanity is essential. The skill of intimacy is to share with others, not to set oneself apart. It's been my observation that newly ordained priests often fail to grasp this imperative, partly out of a desire to not make the same mistakes they've observed priests making in the past, especially in light of the sexual abuse scandals. They seem to believe that maintaining a distance from the laity is a prudent observance of boundaries that were lacking in the past. This is a well-intentioned but mistaken posture. You can't lead if you're distant. Who will follow? Being a priest or pastor means to engage in *intimate* communication: listening, identifying with, resonating (using your own emotional experience), clarifying (what do they mean?), formulating (using your knowledge and intellect), responding, and then leading.

Drawing again on the *Program of Priestly Formation*, "A person of affective maturity [is] someone whose life of feelings is in balance and integrated into thought and values; in other words, *a man of feelings who is not driven by them but who freely lives his life enriched by them*" (183e; emphasis added). For true intimate communication to occur, we need to allow ourselves to resonate, to *feel* what the other person is saying. This requires that we have access to our own wellspring of emotions. Over the years, I have found the most common problem among troubled clergy is poor emotional awareness. And that, in turn, allows insidious processes to get us into trouble. If we don't acknowledge feelings of loneliness, for example, how can we deal with them in a way that proves beneficial?

The Problem with "People Pleasing"

In contrast to differentiating themselves from the laity, some pastors have difficulty saying no. Unfortunately, these so-called "people pleasers" become so time-constrained they neglect their families, friends, hobbies (if they have any), even their spirituality. Social isolation is often the result. On the other hand, clergy who moderate their desire to please typically reserve time for their personal lives without feeling selfish or anxious about disappointing others.

What I've observed is that one's sense of being a "good" person may depend on acceptance by others—on whether one is meeting their needs as *they* judge it. Let me be clear here: If your self-worth depends on others liking you, you're in trouble. As previously mentioned, this means you're attempting to build your self-esteem on an external foundation, and when others don't get what they want, you feel distressed and worthless. Before long, you're developing problems with time management, funds management, and self-esteem.

One solution is learning to live and operate within a world of limits. Translation: instead of saying no to a parishioner, say, "I would love to be able to do that, but we don't have the time (or money or ability) right now." Time management is about saying to someone, "I have an appointment and can't speak to you now, but let's plan to get together this Friday when I can give you the time you deserve."

Managing Confrontation

Difficulty with confrontation is a universal problem among clergy. When confrontation is routinely avoided, passive-aggressive behavior can often take its place. Communication between a pastor and his associate or support staff may devolve into note-writing, interpersonal avoidance, and building of resentment among both parties. Without the ability to manage confrontation, you lose the ability to manage yourself, your staff and other relationships, and interpersonal conflicts. In short, you are unable to collaborate.

All of which begs the question, how are you going to work with others if you cannot resolve conflict? It's naïve to assume that disagreements and misunderstandings won't occur when working with others. Confrontation is essentially a discrepancy between two or more people. Perhaps a staff member didn't perform as expected. Why, then, is this so hard to manage? What do we fear when we think of confronting someone? We fear we will hurt the other person's feelings, or have our own feelings hurt. We fear angering the other person, leading to conflict and the raising of voices. We fear the other person won't like us anymore (a consequence of the aforementioned "people pleasing").

To give a practical example, on several occasions I've come across pastors who have had issues with secretaries they inherited from previous pastors. In one case, not only was the employee not very skilled, but she looked for opportunities to undermine the pastor because of her attachment to his predecessor. And because she had been at her job a long time—in fact, she practically ran the parish—the new pastor feared that firing her would touch off something of a palace revolt. In another case, the parish secretary had poor skills but was such a nice person the new pastor could never bring himself to hurt the employee's feelings.

The upshot? Both secretaries kept their jobs, but with a price. Because the authority of the first pastor was constantly undermined, he became more and more resentful. The second pastor was forced to correct his secretary's mistakes, which meant typing things himself, preparing the church bulletin, and doing other small tasks because it was just easier that way. Given how strapped pastors are for time, you can imagine how unhealthy and intolerable this situation became. Lack of conflict resolution came back to haunt both pastors.

How, then, do we confront people in a productive manner? There are some practical rules of the road. First of all, keep in mind the discrepancy is about the person's actions, not about the person. There is no need to apologize for anything you have said, or to be anguished you may have hurt their feelings. Instead, you should start by reminding them of your positive regard for them and their contribution to the parish. Next, calmly and clearly spell out the issue that divides you—what happened, what you thought was going to happen—working through the discrepancy in a logical way. Most importantly, discuss what your expectations are going forward. If they get upset, that is *their* issue, and you should not respond in kind. To do so would be to surrender control of your emotions to them. Instead, you have a responsibility to understand and clarify why they're upset.

You can start to see how skilled confrontation enables *friendship and collaboration*. It can actually be a relief to others—they now know where you stand and where they stand. When things are unclear, suspicion and anxiety ensue as negativity and fear fill the vacuum. Skillful confrontation is an opportunity for positive feelings and intimate communication.

Accepting Authority

Ask any chancery personnel director or bishop, and they'll tell you that priests who have difficulty with authority are a common problem. Typically, they have a chip on their shoulder, or feel the need to constantly show who is "top dog." An aspect of this is "personalization"—the feeling that everything is a reflection on their worth and status. Another offshoot is to judge the behavior of others through a filter that sees conflict where none exists.

Let me assure you this is a lonely and angry place to be. A healthy priest is one who accepts the authority of others—within limits—to serve the good of the church and its people. The *Program of Priestly Formation* is again instructive here: "A person of affective maturity . . . [is] evident in his ability to live well with authority, in his ability to take direction from another, and in his ability to exercise authority well among his peers, as well as an ability to deal productively with conflict and stress" (183e).

Keeping Social Isolation at Bay

Part of the difficulty of transitioning from the seminary to the "real world" is maintaining a social network. While that might have been easy in the seminary, it changes significantly in the parish, and is even more difficult when you become pastor. You are now in a position of power, and living in a fishbowl. Spending time with one person or group, for example, can appear to be "playing favorites." There are new pressures and problems that demand your attention daily. As a result, socializing may seem like a waste of time and energy. Just closing your door, collapsing in your recliner, and having some time to yourself may seem far more desirable.

This is another "insidious" process (defined as one that causes harm in a way that is gradual and not easily noticed) lying in wait for pastors. Pretty soon people stop calling you because you are always busy—or maybe you stop returning their calls from the comfort of your recliner. If you find yourself on this treadmill, you have entered red-flag territory.

Needing friends is not a weakness. You are human, after all, and you need others to validate your existence. That's why your peers—other pastors and priests—are particularly important. They are supportive, caring, and help keep you in check. If you're having difficulty with an issue or an individual, you need to talk it over with others who understand the nuances and difficulties of your situation. Normally you can't do this with parishioners, for that would be to cede your role as their priest, serving instead as their friend. That is what *boundaries* are about.

Be aware that socializing with peers takes some planning. You already know this if you've tried calling priest friends at the last minute to see if they're available on your day off. They're probably not, which can lead to discouragement and social withdrawal. With a little advance planning, however, you can help ensure you're both free and able to enjoy a relaxing day away from the parish and all its attendant concerns.

Accepting Compliments

Does the following sound familiar? "I hear the one negative comment about my homily, and dismiss the one hundred positive compliments—they're just being nice." Allowing in the positive is part of maintaining self-worth and avoiding false humility. Those who compliment you will instinctively know if you are not receptive to them. Not allowing such compliments in can lead you to pursuing affirmation in other, inappropriate, ways, such as flirting or seeking adulation from parishioners.

Learn how to accept compliments. This is not about pride, but support. As the *Program of Priestly Formation* puts it, "A man of communion . . .

[is] open to others and available to them with a generosity of spirit. The man of communion is capable of making a gift of himself and of receiving the gift of others" (183c).

Accenting the Positive

Like people in any field, priests who dwell on the negative aspects of work, relationships with others, and the world around them generally are destined for a life of misery and stress. As part of your emotional awareness development, ask yourself, Am I looking at the negative side only? What are the positives? Then engage a peer or friend in the discussion. Research shows that dwelling on life's dark and gloomy corners contributes to poor adjustment and early burnout. Furthermore, negative emotions can have a pervasive influence on perceptions and behaviors, so that potentially valuable resources like social and organizational support are never fully appreciated or utilized.

By shifting gears from "learned helplessness" to "learned optimism," the psychologist Martin Seligman developed a program to accentuate the positive. One of his techniques is to think of three good things at the end of each day and write them down in a journal. This exercise should be done during a prearranged quiet period in which you're able to listen to God and to your own heart, and reflect on the events of the day. There will be some days, of course, where things didn't go well, but through a better understanding of *why*, you can make adjustments to ensure the next day is better. Keeping this kind of journal also encourages gratitude and an inner optimism.

I've had priests say to me, "That sounds nice, but I really don't have the time for it." My response to them is, "You owe it to yourself to take the time. If you realize how important it can be to your well-being, you'll find a way to make it happen."

Adjusting to the Priesthood

I've found through my work with priests that those who adjust best to their jobs have an ability to disengage from their demanding roles as leaders. In other words, those who take time to tend to their needs as human beings fare the best. It is not selfish to minister to oneself.[3]

Other traits that can help prevent burnout are a sense of personal autonomy, strong social support, and organizational backing. That's why having a mentor is extremely important. It's your acknowledgment that you can't do it all, that you don't (nor should you) have all the answers, that you don't believe seeking guidance is a sign of weakness.

It's amazing to me that so many priests don't have a spiritual director. We all instinctively know that an internal orientation to spirituality is essential to vocational satisfaction. The danger of not having that focus is for you to turn away from and sacrifice the ingredient that is most vital to your vocation: spirituality. Finding the right spiritual director is not always easy; in fact, it's becoming increasingly difficult. But given the multitude of pressures and distractions that priests confront daily, it's a task you can't afford *not* to undertake.

The Protective Effect of Self-Compassion

A heavy dose of self-compassion can also help ease your journey through priesthood. As discussed by the authors Laura Barnard and John Curry, it can benefit you in three ways. First, by offering you kindness, patience, and understanding during times of failure, stress, or disappointment. Second, by recognizing that others find themselves in similar valleys, and by having self-compassion they are able to feel connected rather than isolated. Third, by allowing you to hold your worries in *mindful awareness* without ruminating on them, you are free to dwell on positive accomplishments rather than be brought down by emotional exhaustion.[4]

Essential to developing self-compassion is spending fifteen to twenty minutes in both the morning and the evening on contemplation (the evening portion could be your journaling exercise, previously discussed). These should be quiet periods in which you listen to God and to your own heart, and reflect on events of the most recent day and the day that lies ahead.

The Importance of Physical Health

It's not uncommon for priests to eschew physical exercise on the following grounds: "Why should I selfishly spend time working out or caring for my own health? That's not serving the people." The answer, of course, is that if you want to have a long and successful priesthood, you need to take care of your physical self. Scientific literature is replete with studies that demonstrate the stress-reducing and resilience-enhancing effects of exercise. To be in shape not only increases stamina, but elevates mood. I know of a number of pastors who have undertaken exercise regimens and reaped tremendous benefits. These include extra stores of energy, motivation, and enthusiasm that bring them "faithfully" to the gym at five in the morning for their daily workouts.

Fighting Addiction through Active Coping

One way to think of addiction is as a compulsion designed to distract us from unpleasant and often painful perceptions of ourselves. It can encompass alcohol abuse, pornography, sex, gambling, overeating, and masturbation. Almost any activity can be done in a compulsive way (without awareness or conscious control) to achieve the goal of emotional denial.

To break the cycle of addiction, we need to adopt an *active* coping style and be able to access our interior lives. That means fighting social isolation and accepting the help of others. It means taking a spiritual "inventory" and discovering how and why we've become disconnected from our spiritual selves. We then need to apply and practice the skills that we've discussed—exercising self-compassion, accenting the positive in your life, accepting support from a mentor/ spiritual director/social network, knowing how to disengage from your pastoral role, taking time for your physical needs—to get back on the right path.

You Owe It to Yourself

As you evolve in your spiritual role as pastor, it's important to recognize the need to grow in other ways as well. There are things you can—and must—do to promote and ensure your wellness. As the *Program of Priestly Formation* points out, social interaction and skills should not be viewed as peripheral to what you do, but as integral to your vocation. By paying attention to and practicing self-care, you can lessen the likelihood of problems and pressures overwhelming you.

An active coping strategy embraces a host of things you can do for yourself to maintain a healthy mind and body. I suggest keeping a "Wellness Checklist" similar to the one that follows to keep you focused in social, spiritual, pastoral, emotional, and physical realms.

Monthly Wellness Checklist

SOCIAL

1. ☐ I called a peer and made a social appointment for some time in the next two weeks.

2. ☐ I called a family member and caught up with the goings on in our family.

3. ☐ I spoke with a friend about my week. I listened to the positive and negative things my friend has been through as well.

4. ☐ I have been mindful of my boundaries with staff and parishioners.

5. ☐ I have been mindful of my feelings and fantasies.

6. ☐ I did not view inappropriate material on my computer this month.

SPIRITUAL

7. ☐ I celebrated Mass and prayed the Office.

8. ☐ I did some spiritual reading.

9. ☐ I prayed the rosary.

10. ☐ I have scheduled a meeting with my spiritual director/confessor within the next month or so.

11. ☐ I prepared for an upcoming day of recollection or annual retreat.

12. ☐ I spent some time before the Blessed Sacrament devoting myself to some one-on-one time with the Lord.

PASTORAL

13. ☐ I have tried to be mindful of my motivations for ministry—it is not in the service of being liked, admired, or adored.

14. ☐ I have been able to be compassionate and understanding with parishioners and staff, modeling kindness whenever I could.

15. ☐ I made a pastoral visit to a parishioner at home or in the hospital.

16. ☐ With compassion and nurturance, I was able to confront someone who needed it.

17. ☐ I maintained an attitude of collaboration with my staff.

EMOTIONAL

18. ☐ I maintained self-compassion.

19. ☐ I looked for, and let go of, resentment.

20. ☐ My mood has been positive; I feel hopeful about the future.

21. ☐ I have felt gratitude for friends and family.

22. ☐ I have been aware of my feelings and did not distract myself from them with work or avoidance.

23. ☐ I did not feel lonely; or, if I did, I tried reaching out to others.

24. ☐ I planned and protected my day off and spent it outside the rectory.

25. ☐ I have spent some good "alone time," allowing myself to decompress and relax.

26. ☐ I have nurtured myself with some activity I enjoy, such as reading a book, watching a movie, focusing on a hobby, etc.

PHYSICAL

27. ☐ I have had a medical checkup within the last year and I am caring for my health by taking my medications and following my doctor's advice.

28. ☐ I did not abuse nicotine, alcohol, food, or other drugs.

29. ☐ I have done 20–30 minutes of daily exercise.

30. ☐ I watched my diet, and have been mindful of my weight.

Essentially, a pastor's wellness is a carefully balanced system, each facet feeding the others. That's why it's not a bad idea to sit down at the end of each day and take stock of what happened. It should be a quiet period in which you may listen to God and to your own heart and reflect on the events of the day.

I also suggest writing down three things that went well, and why. There will be some days that don't go well, of course. We've all had them, and there's nothing wrong with acknowledging it. But through a better understanding of why they occurred, we can take steps to ensure that the next day is sunnier, that we're better able to deal with the drumbeat of issues and the people around us from a position of confidence and strength.

In conclusion, a point that bears repeating, as I have found it to be so beneficial in the health and wellness of priests, is that you owe it to yourself to take the time to do these things. If you realize how critical it is to your well-being, you'll find a way to make it happen.

Endnotes

1. "Address of His Holiness Pope Francis to Participants in the Convention Sponsored by the Congregation for the Clergy on the 50th Anniversary of the Conciliar Decrees *Optatam Totius* and *Presbyterorum Ordinis*," November 20, 2015, https://w2.vatican.va/content/francesco/en/speeches/2015/november/documents /papa-francesco_20151120_formazione-sacerdoti.html.

2. USCCB, *Program of Priestly Formation*, 6th ed. (Washington, DC: USCCB, 2022).

3. D. K. Pooler, "Pastors and Congregations at Risk: Insights from Role Identity Theory," *Pastoral Psychology* 60 (October 2011).

4. Laura Barnard and John Curry, "The Relationship of Clergy Burnout to Self-Compassion and Other Personality Dimensions," *Pastoral Psychology* 61, no. 2 (April 2012).

Contributors

Michael Brough serves as an executive partner of Leadership Roundtable, working with senior Catholic executives and church leaders to promote best practices in church management and leadership. In his more than thirty years of professional ministry in the Catholic Church, Michael has worked with and trained lay ecclesial ministers, priests, and bishops in dioceses and parishes across the United States and in thirteen different countries. He has also served as a consultant to Catholic nonprofits, boards, foundations, and other institutions. Michael developed Leadership Roundtable's Catholic Standards for Excellence program and is certified by the Center for Creative Leadership to deliver the Catholic Leadership 360 assessment tool. He is a faculty member for the Toolbox for Pastoral Management and is the author of chapters on leadership and best practices in both volumes of *A Pastor's Toolbox* (Liturgical Press, 2014, 2017).

Dennis Cheesebrow has more than twenty years of serving the education, faith, government, business, and human service marketplaces. He brings broad experience in coaching, consulting, leadership, and systems development. Clients appreciate his direct style sprinkled with humor, and a deep appreciation for human dynamics and potential. In the Catholic Church, Dennis served on many councils and committees. He also developed and facilitated diocesan-wide pastoral and Catholic school planning initiatives, assessment and redesign of diocesan offices and consultative structures, and operational assessment, improvement, and transition management services. Through individualized coaching, he has supported pastors, principals, and ministry directors. In 2012, Dennis authored the book *Partnership: Redefined; Leadership through the Power of "&"* as well as the *Educational Leadership System Guidebook* (2009) and the *FrameWorks Guidebook* (2009). He was a contributing author to the book *Voices from the Field: An Introduction to Human Systems Dynamics* in 2003. He holds three US patents from his seventeen years at 3M as an engineer, research laboratory manager, and marketing/business manager before founding TeamWorks International, Inc.

Barbara Anne Cusack is chancellor of the Archdiocese of Milwaukee and has been a judge and promoter of justice for various courts in Milwaukee, Chicago, and the province of Illinois. She has participated in research groups for a number of committees of the Canon Law Society of America and the United States Conference of Catholic Bishops. Barbara has lectured and published widely, including "Relationship between the Diocesan Bishop and Catholic Schools," "The Role of Laity in the Church," *Pastoral Care in Parishes without a Pastor*, "Diocesan Structures," and "'In Communion with the Church' as Applied to Catholic Health Care." She has also been a canonical advisor and contributor to the Leadership Roundtable's Catholic Standards for Excellence.

Jesuit Father Allan Figueroa Deck is a distinguished scholar in pastoral theology and Latino studies and holds a dual appointment as lecturer in the departments of theological studies and Chicano/Latino/a studies at Loyola Marymount University. He earned doctoral degrees in theology from the Pontifical Gregorian University and in Latin American studies from Saint Louis University. Father Deck is the author or editor of nine books and more than sixty chapters in books and journal articles on pastoral theology, Latino/a studies, Catholic social teaching, spirituality and intercultural competence. Father Deck's latest book is *Francis, Bishop of Rome: The Gospel for the Third Millennium* (Paulist Press, 2016). In addition to teaching, research, and writing, Father Deck has served as parish administrator, director of Hispanic ministry, founder and first executive director of the Loyola Institute for Spirituality in Orange, California, and cofounder and first president of the Academy of Catholic Hispanic Theologians of the United States (ACHTUS). He served as first executive director of the Secretariat of Cultural Diversity in the Church of the United States Conference of Catholic Bishops. A nationally recognized speaker, Father Deck has received the John XXIII Award of the Catholic Library Association for contributions to church renewal in the spirit of the Second Vatican Council, the Sadlier Award for contributions to religious education, and the Virgilio Elizondo Award of ACHTUS for contributions to the development of a theology of and for Latino/as in the United States.

Peter Denio serves as program manager for Leadership Roundtable, facilitating leadership formation programs and providing overall administration of several of Leadership Roundtable's programs including the Toolbox for Pastoral Management, Catholic Leadership 360, and Catholic Standards for Excellence. He has worked nationally at leadership formation organizations that serve the Catholic Church and locally in parish ministry as a lay ecclesial minister for more than thirty years. He is currently on the advisory board of the Catholic Common Ground Initiative. Peter also currently serves as a pastoral associate for adult faith formation at a parish in New Jersey. He is certified by the Center for Creative Leadership to deliver the Catholic Leadership 360 assessment tool and is a certified Standards for Excellence licensed consultant. Peter serves as a faculty member for the Toolbox for Pastoral Management and is the author of a chapter on meeting management in *A Pastor's Toolbox 2* (Liturgical Press, 2017).

James M. Dubik is a retired army general, former infantryman, paratrooper, and ranger. He holds a PhD in philosophy from Johns Hopkins University and has published over 150 essays and monographs. He is coauthor of *Envisioning Future Warfare* and author of *Just War Reconsidered: Strategy, Ethics, and Theory* (University Press of Kentucky, 2016). James serves on the board and as trustee of the Leadership Roundtable. He is a member of the Council on Foreign Relations, an inductee of the US Army Ranger Hall of Fame, and a distinguished member of the US Army 75th Ranger Regiment. He was the 2012–13 General Omar N. Bradley Chair in Strategic Leadership cosponsored by Dickinson College, the United States Army War College, and Penn State Law school.

Carol Fowler was director of the department of personnel services for the Archdiocese of Chicago (1991–2012), coordinating the work of fourteen archdiocesan agencies that oversaw all human resources functions for the fifteen thousand laity, religious, and clergy of the archdiocese. Carol was president of the National Association of Church Personnel Administrators and has been a member of the board of the Leadership Roundtable. She was also a member of the advisory board of the Center for the Study of Church Management at Villanova University. Holding a DMin from St. Mary's Seminary and University in Baltimore as well as an MA in counseling psychology from the Adler School of Professional Psychology, she is a senior professional in human resources, certified by the Institute of the

Society for Human Resource Management. Carol continues to share her wisdom with her most recent book, *Human Resources: Best Practices in Church Management* (Paulist Press, 2019).

Father Cesar Izquierdo is a priest of the Diocese of Yakima and was ordained to the priesthood on July 3, 2018, at Christ the King Parish in Richland, Washington State. He is the pastor of St. Rose of Lima Parish and School. Originally from Mexico, he emigrated with his family to Washington State at the age of seventeen. He holds a licentiate in philosophy from the Lumen Gentium University in Mexico City, a baccalaureate in theology from the Angelicum University, and a licentiate in public ethics and social doctrine of the church from the Gregorian University in Rome. Father Cesar was first assigned to St. Joseph's Parish in Kennewick as associate pastor and then as parish administrator. During his studies in Rome, he did ministry at the Shrine of the Immaculate Conception in Naples, Italy, and at Saint Peter's Parish in London. He also volunteered with International Charities at Casa di Iqbal Refugee Center and provided document translations at the Synod of Bishops for the Pan-Amazon Region in 2018–2019. He enjoys doing radio presentations and interviews and has done broadcasting at Vatican Radio during the international apostolic visits of Pope Francis, and has also contributed with translation and commentary for the Sunday Angelus with the Holy Father from 2017 to 2020. Most recently Father Cesar collaborates with Korgen Associates in the Servant Leadership Program.

Andrew F. Kelly has served as director of Clergy Consultation and Treatment Service at St. Vincent's Hospital in Harrison, New York. For more than twenty years, he was both the clinical and administrative director of this multidisciplinary outpatient treatment program for priests, both diocesan and religious, in both individual and group modalities. He also served as clinical assistant professor of psychiatry at New York Medical College. Dr. Kelly lives in New York City. He is an accomplished diagnostician, therapist, and aftercare specialist, assisting clergy in developing healthy responses to the difficult and rewarding challenges of priestly ministry.

Rev. Dr. Kevin C. Kennedy serves as a senior leadership director with Leadership Roundtable and is a faculty member for the Toolbox for Pastoral Management and accompanies parish and diocesan leaders in developing their capacity to thrive and lead effectively. Kevin is a Standards for Excellence licensed consultant, certified to use the Immunity to Change™ change management process, and is certified by the Center for Creative Leadership to deliver the Catholic Leadership 360 assessment tool. He has twenty-seven years of pastoral experience at seven parishes in the Archdiocese of Washington and served as a dean (vicar forane) in three deaneries. For fifteen years, he taught graduate courses in organizational development and leadership at The Catholic University of America. Prior to ordination, Kevin worked in the capital markets and corporate finance.

Jim Lundholm-Eades serves as senior consultant and, until his retirement, served as Leadership Roundtable's director of programs and services. He has worked with over one hundred dioceses and archdioceses, many religious orders, and national Catholic organizations. He has been a national speaker, university faculty member, researcher, and author on diocesan administration, deep culture change in dioceses, pastoral leadership strategies, clergy assignment for dioceses, church finance, pastoral planning, and how dioceses and parishes recover from sexual abuse. Jim has coached senior church leaders including cardinals, bishops, and vicars generals. Previously he served as director of parish services and planning and was the associate director of Catholic education in the Archdiocese of St. Paul and Minneapolis. Jim has graduate degrees in educational administration, pastoral counseling, counseling, and business administration. Prior to his retirement he was licensed as a school superintendent. Jim is certified to deliver the Catholic Leadership 360 assessment tool.

Patrick Markey, CPA, MBA, serves as managing partner of Leadership Roundtable, overseeing operations and personnel. Before joining Leadership Roundtable, he spent seven years as executive director of the Diocesan Fiscal Management Conference (DFMC). Patrick also has worked at the United States Conference of Catholic Bishops (USCCB). He is a certified public accountant and holds an executive MBA degree from the University of Loyola in Baltimore. He also has completed other graduate studies in theology at Fordham University. He has served on the boards of the Catholic Volunteer Network, the Center for Ministry Development, New City Press, and the John 17 Movement. He is a consultant to the USCCB's Committee on National Collections, Subcommittee on the Church in Africa, and Subcommittee on Aid to the Church in Central and Eastern Europe.

John McGovern is a licensed CPA, holds the designation of personal financial specialist, and is also a certified financial planner and a registered investment advisor with the Securities and Exchange Commission. He began his career with Deloitte and Touche, and in 1986 opened his accounting practice specializing in the areas of tax, investment management, and church accounting. Currently, John provides accounting services to thirty parishes, cemeteries, and parish schools.

Jeffry Odell Korgen serves as a Leadership Roundtable consultant. As president of Korgen Associates, he is a writer and church consultant who provides coaching, planning, and evaluation services to Catholic and interfaith organizations, including serving as coordinator of Cardinal Dolan's Inquiry into the Life and Virtues of Dorothy Day. Jeff previously served as executive director for the department of diocesan planning for the Diocese of Metuchen and as director of social ministries for the National Pastoral Life Center. Prior to that, he worked as a youth minister and as lead organizer for the Brockton Interfaith Community of the Massachusetts Community Action Network. He received an MA in pastoral ministry, a master of social work, and a BA from Boston College. He is certified by the Center for Creative Leadership to deliver the Catholic Leadership 360 assessment tool and is a faculty member for the Toolbox for Pastoral Management.

Helen Osman, president of Greater Wings, LLC, has thirty plus years of experience in mentoring mission-focused organizations to integrate public awareness, catechetical expectations, and advocacy priorities. While her clients range from highly localized to international in scope, a specialty is providing communication strategies for Roman Catholic parishes and dioceses. Helen has worked in communications for faith-based organizations since 1984, shortly after she moved to Central Texas with her husband, John. They returned to Austin in November 2015, after an eight-year hiatus in Washington, DC, where she coordinated communications for the US Catholic bishops and shepherded the visits to the United States of Pope Benedict XVI in 2008 and Pope Francis in 2015. She serves as a consultor to the Dicastery for Communications, is president of the international board for SIGNIS, the World Catholic Association for Communications, and is a member of the board for the American Bible Society.

Nicole M. Perone is the National Coordinator of ESTEEM, the faith-based leadership formation program for Catholic students at colleges and universities across the United States. She holds an MDiv from Yale University and a BA in theology from Loyola University Maryland. Nicole previously served as the archdiocesan director of adult faith formation for the Archdiocese of Hartford. Nicole is the chair of the Board of Governors for the National Institute for Ministry with Young Adults, and on the writing team for the US Conference of Catholic Bishops' pastoral framework on youth and young adult ministry. She is a member of the National Advisory Council for the NeXt Level initiative of the Center for FaithJustice and the Advisory Board of the Youth in the 21st Century Initiative of Sacred Heart University, as well as the Board of Trustees for Our Lady of Calvary Retreat Center. Nicole was a delegate to the Vatican Pre-Synod on Young People, the Faith, and Vocational Discernment, and served on the writing committee for the final document. Her work has been published by *America Media*, *Catholic News Service*, *The Jesuit Post*, and *U.S. Catholic*.

Dominic Perri serves as senior leadership consultant and has worked with more than two thousand priests and one hundred organizations in more than twenty-five dioceses providing strategic planning services and leadership development. Dominic serves as a consultant to the USCCB Committee on Communications. Dominic has extensive experience working as a researcher at the Survey Research Center at the University of Maryland-College Park and the Center for Applied Research in the Apostolate (CARA) at Georgetown University. He is certified by the Center for Creative Leadership to deliver the Catholic Leadership 360 assessment tool, is a certified Covey 7 Habits Trainer, trained in DiSC® Profile, and Neurolinguistic Programming. Dominic received a BS in physics from The Catholic University of America. He also has an MA in sociology and an MA in economics from the University of Maryland. He is the author of a chapter on developing a pastoral vision in *A Pastor's Toolbox 2* (Liturgical Press, 2017).

Father Anthony J. Pogorelc is a Sulpician priest and has held faculty and administrative positions in seminaries in Washington, DC, Menlo Park, California, and San Antonio, Texas. He holds an MDiv from St. Michael's College of the University of Toronto, an STL from St. Mary's Seminary and University, Baltimore, and a PhD in sociology from Purdue University. Specializing in the sociology of religion, his research has focused on social movements and organizations, young adults and professional ministers. He is a member of the American Sociological Association (ASA), the Society for the Scientific Study of Religion (SSSR), the Association for the Sociology of Religion (ASR), and the Religious Research Association (RRA). He currently serves as provincial secretary, director of personnel, and director of initial formation at the Society of St. Sulpice, US Province in Baltimore.

Kerry Alys Robinson is president and CEO of Catholic Charities USA. She previously served as an executive partner at Leadership Roundtable. She is a member of the Raskob Foundation for Catholic Activities and FADICA (Foundations and Donors Interested in Catholic Activities). Kerry is the director of the Opus Prize Foundation, responsible for an annual international million-dollar prize honoring people of faith whose ministry is dedicated to the alleviation of human suffering. She has been an advisor to and trustee of more than twenty-five national and international grant-making foundations and charitable nonprofits. Prior to Leadership Roundtable, Kerry served as the director of development for Saint Thomas More Catholic Chapel and Center at Yale University where she led a successful $75 million capital campaign to expand and endow the Chapel's intellectual and spiritual ministry and to construct a Catholic student center. A frequent writer and international speaker, Kerry is the prize-winning author of *Imagining Abundance: Fundraising, Philanthropy, and a Spiritual Call to Service* (Liturgical Press, 2014). Kerry has been a columnist for *Chicago Catholic* since 2017. She is a graduate of Georgetown and Yale.

Deacon Patrick Stokely is a senior program manager at Leadership Roundtable delivering the full suite of leadership formation programs and consultancy services. He has facilitated leadership formation for Catholic clergy and lay leaders throughout the United States and Canada for over twenty years. Patrick has a wide range of experience in both corporate and faith-based environments, including serving in significant sales and marketing leadership positions at AT&T and Verizon. He has extensive experience in analysis and organizational design working with bishops and their leadership teams. Patrick is certified by the Center for Creative Leadership to deliver the Catholic Leadership 360 assessment tool, is a certified Standards for Excellence licensed consultant, and is certified in the DiSC® Profile. He also serves on the faculty for the Toolbox for Pastoral Management. Patrick is a permanent deacon and serves in the Archdiocese of Philadelphia.